ROCK BOTTOM, THEN UP AGAIN

AND OTHER SPIRITUAL ESSAYS

To Mollye Courts!,

Great seeing you
in the hallways
each day!,

[signature]

FROM THE AUTHOR OF

FUNNY CONVERSATIONS WITH GOD – AN UNCALLED-FOR DIALOGUE

ROCK
BOTTOM,
THEN UP AGAIN

AND OTHER SPIRITUAL ESSAYS

DUNN NEUGEBAUER

MOUNTAIN ARBOR PRESS

Mountain Arbor
Press
Alpharetta, GA

ISBN: 978-1-63183-442-4 - Paperback
eISBN: 978-1-63183-443-1 - ePub
eISBN: 978-1-63183-444-8 - Mobi

Library of Congress Control Number: 2018962085

10 9 8 7 6 5 4 3 2   1 0 2 3 1 8

Printed in the United States of America

♾This paper meets the requirements of ANSI/NISO Z39.48-1992
(Permanence of Paper)

Front and back cover photos by Julie Fennell

Acknowledgements

A book doesn't write itself, and as always – it takes more than just the author to put one to bed. Special thanks to Pride Evans and Skip Johnson for putting up with my constant barrage of essays for them to look over.

They not only took the time, but their honest comments, criticisms and suggestions were more than helpful in putting this together. Words can't express my appreciation and – when we all get together again – the first round is on Skip.

Peggy Shaw deserves a lot of credit in all this, not only for the professional edit, but for reminding me that of all the jobs I have at school, continuing to write is one of them. Julie Fennell's photography is and was also appreciated; she did a great job considering her subject.

My girlfriend, Sheryl, also deserves some love here. Being on dates with someone who's writing a book is not always an easy thing – love to her for being patient when I drifted off into 'author land.' As Billy Joel once sang, "When I'm deep inside of me, don't be too concerned. I won't ask for nothing while I'm gone." She gets that, not all do. Thanks.

I also want to thank the students, faculty, staff, and parents at Holy Innocents', mainly just for being themselves. Being in energetic hallways with full speed adrenaline is constantly a source of gratitude for me – I feed off this almost every day of my life. It starts early with carpool and doesn't end until late at night with collecting the scores.

Still, when you'd do what you do for free, you've got yourself a pretty good gig. My thanks to the entire place for putting up with me.

Finally, to anyone who reads this: If nothing else, I hope the following words of this book inspire you and move you to peace, to finding and doing what you love, and to living your best self. I've shared in my words of times when I was less than my best, and of my continuing education to present day.

I also hope the words teach you there is strength in vulnerability; in fact, that's where all the education and adventures are. As someone once wrote, comfort zones are nice, but nothing ever grows there.

Peace, always peace!

Contents

First, Something I Need to Tell You...

A couple years ago – filled with the writings of great authors and the inspiration from running at a nearby park – I decided it was time to pen the Great American Novel. After all, I wasn't getting any younger, most of the writing I was doing was compiling and writing sports stories, and, being around high school kids every day, I had plenty of material.

So, one day I sat down. Do I do this in diary fashion like "Be True to Your School" by Bob Greene? Or make it a mystery novel where I can become the next Harlan Coben? Another self-help book – though my shelves were and are already crammed?

Two things happened: First, I read somewhere you should write the book you'd like to read. Second, I got the idea to simply write an essay or two until I got going on THE NOVEL.

One year and 87 essays later, I read back over my massive words and figured maybe I was on to something. And yes, it came down to a heavy influence on two questions – who am I, and what do I like to read?

I'm into spirituality, humor, and sports; I like to read, write, and run. It's who I am, what I do, what I want to be remembered for. In looking over these essays, most of them contain some of the above – while others do stray.

Without taking up more of your time, what follows are true-to-life, from-the-heart briefs, penned for no other reason than the fact they were what I had to say. I was tired of reading other people's opinions; even more tired of political rants on Facebook, so this is my attempt to offset that if you will; provide some light and peace.

Also, and as I've read, this world is getting better and worse at the same time. Which side do I want to contribute to? Again, who am I?

In moving on, some of these are nostalgic – good for me. All of them mean well. None are coaxing you into any sort of presidential candidate or religious belief.

What follows will take you back, bring you forward and hopefully, just hopefully, make you enjoy your life journey just a little bit more. After all, every little bit helps.

Lastly, my roles as teacher, coach, friend, and writer are to assist, leave you feeling a little lighter when you walk away. These stories are my invitation to approach. One rule, though: Come to me in peace. After all, that's the way all these essays were written.

Dunn Neugebauer
Summer, 2018

"One day I will find the right words, and they will be simple."
—Jack Kerouac

And Sometimes 'Y'

MADISON, GA, 1966 - I was a 6-year-old boy and I was going to be a star! After all, this was the week of the big play, "The Vowels," and I was the "A"! "It was A, E, I, O, U, and sometimes Y; "happy little monkeys swinging up so high." That was the song – we even had a song! And I had the opening part!

I would dance across that stage, hold my prized letter, speak my lines, then strut before the rest of those vowels, daring them to upstage me, give them something to envy. Too young to know there was no "I" in team, all I knew was there was an "M" and an "E." Right then, that meant me!

Then… disaster struck. My drama teacher had a change of plans; gave my part to Terry Armstead. I was now the "Y." From the star, to the silent vowel. Such pain to put on a first-grader. Could I do it?

The curtains opened; Terry flubbed one of his lines. I think it's because I put the Ninja Curse on him – though not sure that existed at the time. Me, I quietly held my "Y", walked across the stage. Hearing my mother's voice even then – "Be nice!" – I did not stick my tongue out at Terry, nor did I give him the dreaded evil eye.

Walking silently, I left the stage since I was only a "sometimes Y", not even a real vowel. Star? I wasn't even real! I choked down tears as I sang about those (bleeping) monkeys; went home, played Chutes and Ladders; dug in the closet to find my

Lite Brite. Pathetic really, to have your hopes and dreams dashed before you've grown your first zit; had your first filling.

WEST PALM BEACH, FL, 2005 – It was Amateur Night at the Improv. Disguised as a married man and not doing very well at it, I had not much else to do. I wrote my script, entered, knew my audience. With the area filled with retirees often playing golf, I had a "can't miss" mixture of jokes about life on the links. I would start with some simple ones before delivering a line that's never failed – the one about the guy swinging and missing the whole ball on the first hole; then looking at me and saying, "Man, this is a tough course!"

I had told that joke 250 times, had gotten a laugh every time. Except this one. Nothing. Not a word, not a giggle, not even a polite golf clap. Broken and stunned, I muttered some more, walked off the stage, went home to a disappointed wife. No Chutes and Ladders in sight; a wonderful zit and an egg, though, still on my face.

ATLANTA, GA, 2018: I've accepted my karma and I love it – it's all about passion and loving what you do anyway. Recently, I've signed on to be the "Sometimes Y" at Holy Innocents' for another year. I'll make few decisions but I will support, clap, cheer. I've outgrown my zits, had my fillings, played my board games.

Yesterday I helped someone with a speech, today subbed for Michelsen while he was stuck in traffic; filled in for DeSantis when he went off to baseball. Support. Passion. I've learned people love passion, will stand and cheer for it after a talk no matter your role.

Still, whether they stand and cheer for me isn't the point anymore anyway. I no longer have to be the happy little monkey swinging up so high.

Because I get to be the one holding the rope.

The 8, 8, 8 Test

I think God answers us through our gut. When we don't listen, we lose.

I feel called to write this because of a conversation I've had over the years, about 2,000 times. "I'm doing this for a living, but I want to be doing that." Or "Man, I would LOVE to somehow make that work."

Get the picture: In the 80s, I was disguised as a banker. I sat and "checked credit" for the unsuspecting public. Though I was supposed to be looking at D&B reports and bank histories, my decision would come down to something like this: They seem so nice! I don't want to kill their dream. Of course, our fine company will loan you $50,000!

My boss was never impressed with this; he quickly knew I was a duck out of water. So, one night I went home and gave myself the "8, 8, 8" test. If you hate your job, the first eight hours of the day are screwed, hence, your next eight, when you're off and tooling around, is also out the door because you're griping about the first eight. "Wow," I thought, "this is a really horrible way to be living!" The final eight, you're asleep so you're unconscious anyway.

Summation: I successfully failed the '8' test. And with flying colors.

One day I got an offer that woke up my hibernating stomach. See, at the bank the only thing I looked forward to was the end of the month newsletter I wrote. Politically correct hadn't yet reared its ugly head, so I let it fly. (Eventually I'd be shut down for my candor). Regardless, what fun! Also, the first day I saw people laughing at what I wrote, I was hooked. Something pounded at my stomach; the Heavens popped me on my thick skull.

In moving on, a newspaper offered me a job. The pay was lower than ridiculous. The hours were and still are seven days a week. I'd travel around with a gas tank nearly empty and I'd perhaps be the only person in the stands. There was a decent chance not even the players' parents would read what I wrote.

Did I want the job? "Son, you have the weekend to think about it." Did I want to do this – complete with 10-grand pay cut? Was I crazy? Fortunately, I am a bit, so this is what I did:

I used Saturday as if I'd already decided to stay at the bank. How did I feel that day? Was I happy? Did I have an extra spring in my step? The answers, in all cases, were a unanimous no!

Sunday, I acted as if I was going to be a sportswriter. I pictured myself banging away at the keyboards whether anyone read what I wrote or not. And if no one did, I'd be selfish enough to write just for me. How did I feel that day? Was I happy? Yes, I was! More than wonderful! More than alive! Excited!

Monday, I walked into the bank and resigned. My boss said, "Thank God!" (he actually didn't but I'm good at reading body language). And finally, here's the thing: Within a year, even the money was made up, or often gets made up. After all, when you're making contacts at what you hate to do, so what? Do you want another job doing what you hate?

Conversely, when you make contacts doing what you love, they are great, exciting. You're in the arena with people of common interests. Before long, there were plenty of writing jobs on the side for magazines and papers, which kept me around sports people who led to me to writing/coaching/speaking.

And to think, making the bank/writer decision was tough that weekend. Looking at the whole picture, I figure challenges are ahead no matter what you do. On bad days, when I wonder if I made the right call, if the words won't come or I wonder if they matter, I let the thoughts go, sit back and smile.

After all, the gut doesn't lie.

I Confess, I Forgive

Confession and forgiveness are good for the soul. Besides, if I want to live a life depending on karma to even things out, then I want to be on the good side. With that said:

To my college buddy Fred: Sorry I left you when I was driving the getaway car. Still, and in my defense, by definition the car was supposed to get away. And it did... just sayin...

To the angry boyfriend that entered that 3rd floor Morton Lemley college dorm with my wide-eyed 18-year-old self in there: I didn't touch her! Don't remember if it's because she wouldn't let me or I didn't try, but I swear I didn't touch her.

To the doctor who told me my right leg would be okay, only to find out later they almost had to amputate: I rolled my ankle the other day and, because of you, I was grateful it was there in the first place. So, thanks, I think.

To the motorcycle gang I faced armed only with an ink pen and a Berry tennis jacket: Thanks for not killing me. And, for the record, it was Hugh's fault...

To the dentist who pulled out one of my wisdom teeth using very little Novocain: Damn, what did they teach you in dental school?

To the driver that hit me in our head-on collision down in Hilton Head: All I want for Christmas is my two front teeth. Seriously...

To the driver who tried to outrun the police with me in the passenger seat: Were you high? Though I guess I should thank you, God and I got REALLY close while you were speeding.

To the editor of a pro sports magazine that let me go: You are easy to forgive – now I get to write about some of the best kids on the planet. Sorry Chipper Jones and Dave Justice, but I get to write about Skye Bolt, Bryn Foster and Blake Morain – to name only some. Gotcha!!!

To my oldest brother: I'm sorry I stole your baseball cards. There was a 1975 Freddie Patek card sitting right on top of the stack – in non-mint condition. How could I resist? He was a lifetime .239 hitter!

To my older brother: Sorry I celebrated when you totaled my car and I forgot to ask if you were okay. Something about that 1969 Ford Falcon that brought out the worst in me.

To Mom: Sorry I was responsible for the only time I ever heard you cuss in my life. Still, if you're 8 and a beach ball is in front of you, you simply must kick it! Sorry about the chandelier, though.

To my high school coaches: Sorry but I did warn you up front when I said, "I may be little but I sure am slow." Also, you asked if I played any sports and I said, "Not athletically." That should've been enough but still…

To my college doubles partner, the one I hit in the back of the head with both my first and second serve: That was hilarious! Besides, it couldn't have hurt! My serves could never have even gotten a speeding ticket!

To the Shoney's manager in Athens: Sorry I walked out without paying. Please send the bill to Bo Slaughter. It was his turn to pay anyway.

To the guy in high school who stole my girlfriend: Now, you have her. See, I win!

And finally, to the people who read my stuff on Facebook: In my defense, I get bored and my computer is right in front of me… right there! Besides, do you want me to start writing politics? That's what I thought.

Have a great day!

The First Step

You've got to crank your car before the GPS kicks in. You must push the keys before the computer responds. You have to press a button on your cell phone before you call somebody.

Somewhere along the line, people were taught to wait. After all, everything must be perfect, the stars must be aligned, the moon must be tilted just so. Nope. It never is. You must go first.

We live in a "when/then" society. When I get the raise, then we'll go here. When I get the girl, we'll go there. When I get the time, I'll do that.

My thoughts: You've got to stand on the starting line before you can compete in the race. You've got to pen the first word before you can write a book. This sounds intimidating, but if you write one page a day for a year, you've got two books, with not that much effort.

It's all about setting the wheels in motion, nothing more. If you don't - if you sit and you wait - then fear sets in. Followed by paralysis. Then, it's nothing more than what might have been. If only…

I was paralyzed for two years of my life. I waited on God, conditions, the right weather, the right bank account, Braves baseball, or whatever, before I was going to make my move. Finally, ticked off at myself, I moved anyway.

Then, Holy Innocents' Episcopal School happened, and I've been kissing the earth it's built on ever since.

Martin Luther would've been proud. After all, I didn't see the whole staircase, I just took the first step. Jumped and the net appeared. Started the web and God sent thread.

And one day, as scared as I was, I sent her a Facebook friend request.

See? I went first.

And you should too.

Just sayin'…

The Art of 5 Getting Dumped

I specifically remember the moment I knew I was a clueless individual. My college girlfriend and I were having "the talk" – which went something like this: "Next year, I'm going to get my master's degree, then I'm going to apply to grad school, probably at Georgia. After that I'm going to get my career going in counseling. What are you going to do?"

I looked her square in the eyes and said, "It's Thursday; I'll probably go to the Pub at about 9:30." Wrong! Ding! Thanks for playing. And even I knew it was over when she said those ominous six words. "Sit down. We need to talk."

With my philosophy etched in stone, I went on to master the art of getting dumped. Perhaps I was a pro if they made such distinctions. On odd Sundays, I can still picture my dejected self, sitting at that Foosball table at the Pub on quarter night. Or over on John Davenport Drive at Discomania 2000. Maybe she was dancing with somebody else. Maybe she preferred sticking needles in both her eyes. It wasn't me, mind you, it was her. (Greatest lie since "Just kidding").

Getting back to said Foosball table, a guy I didn't know very well came over – pulled me aside, sat me down. He was already a worldly fellow, 19 at the mature level of a 100-year old. Me, 20 going on 10. This lad took the time to reach out to someone he barely knew. He didn't give me a choice about getting back up, he pulled me up by my sweaty T-shirt.

I saw this guy again 35 years later at Schroeder's Deli at a Berry class reunion. He was sitting with his clan; I walked past headed for mine. We just pointed to each other, the way basketball players do after a good pass. It was a neat moment, and again made me realize sometimes words are the least effective way to communicate.

Moving to present day, and without being too touchy-feely: In early spring, there's love in the air at the school where I spend my days. I read the lesson plan in class, the girls open their laptops and search for prom dresses. Boys wait nervously by the girls' lockers, ready to pop the question. It's that daring and caring time, and every year I can't help but feed off that energy, feeling happy, depressed and in-between.

Personally, I'm walking light these days. During tough times, I can hear my girlfriend's laughter ringing inside my head, that guffaw thing she does, and it ranks right up there with angels singing and my mother's iced tea. I'm grateful I kept getting off that deck; reminds me to give ourselves credit when we feel the fear and do it anyway. Wear it like a medal, I say. Flex it like a muscle.

My summation: This world needs more caring, not less. Rod Stewart sang about loving in vain; I don't believe there is such a thing - it's as fictional as the Tooth Fairy. See, when you care about something or someone, I can't help but think you're moving the world forward, if only a little.

Smile. Be kind anyway. Show them your best. Write your story. Paint your picture. Kick ass, and I mean that peacefully.

So, cheers to my college comrade from 35 years ago. My spirit wants to pull the boy aside once he doesn't get the answer he was hoping for. I want to tell him that, if nothing else, rejection teaches you how to be a better you. It's taught me how to work at my school and in a more able way. Keep the peaceful energy moving forward. God, we need this now!

New set of downs. Move the chains. First and 10. Regret not one second of the game. With this said, I'll leave you with the two words you've been taught not to believe.

Trust me...

If We Only Knew

I think that instead of meeting our maker and realizing how powerless we were down here on earth; I believe we'll be told the opposite. We didn't know the strength we had, the power of our thoughts, the power of our words.

I think it was Shakespeare who wrote about sticks and stones breaking our bones but words never hurting us. I couldn't carry his typewriter, not a key on it, but I don't agree.

Our words, and the words of others, hurt us every day of our lives. And yes, we are that powerful. I share Wayne Dyer's philosophy: "As a wave is a part of the ocean, we, too, are a part of God."

Point to be made: Watch what you say, particularly when talking about yourself. Your words are prophetic. And if you want changes, write them down! Words are a contract with the Heavens. And to get even more weird, don't type the list. Write it! It should go from your heart to your hand to the paper.

This is powerful, it tells the Gods, the heavens, and the angels you are serious.

When the time comes, I think He'll let us know it was not only as plain as the nose on our faces, but clear in our voices as well. It's a co-creation thing; we just have to remember who the head "co" is.

I believe self-talk is more underrated than drool-generated naps, laughter, water, and the remote control. It should be hyped more than the Super Bowl, prom, the Oscars and the Royal Wedding combined.

As self-deprecating as I am, I've learned to simply shut up. When in doubt, I reach for a pen. The things that matter to me are written on 4 X 6 yellow note cards – with gratitude in advance. (Gratitude in advance: yes, I'm sure I read that somewhere.) I carry the notes in my back pocket; the only time they've missed is when something better came along.

Ask and you shall receive. All these things and more can you do. Seems I've read that somewhere, too.

So, who are we? Do we just read this stuff or do we put it into play? Are they just words?

And if they are just words, I guess that's okay, too. After all, words are incredibly powerful...

Watch what you say; have a good day...

On the Eighth Day, God Created Prom

I'm subbing in physics the day before prom. At one table are five girls, engaged, intense, words flying. It's a huddle with five quarterbacks. They have SO much to address. Hair. Dresses. Nails. Shoes. Seating arrangements. After party. If this were football, they'd be flagged for delay of game 637 times. No worries, they'd ignore the ref and keep talking.

Two feet away are three boys – also going to prom. One of them is asleep. The other is doing calculus. The third on his cell phone, playing games. The sleeping one stirs, looks at me. "What are your pre-prom preparations," I ask. He yawns, "Give me ten minutes to get ready. Tops."

I'm reminded of a scene from *Friends*, after Ross kissed Rachel the first time. The girls heard the news and were excitingly yakking about it in the coffee shop. "Details! Please! Were his arms around you? How did he hold you? Was it a long kiss? What was it like?"

Cut to the three guys at Chandler's place, playing Foosball, with the following conversation between Joey and Ross.

"You kissed Rachel?"

"Yup."

"Tongue?"

"Yup."

"Cool."

The Foosball game never stopped before, during or after the conversation.

It's probably good, this "girls different from guys" thing. Think of it this way: What if both hit their sexual peaks at the same time? My GPA proves I'm no genius, but I still maintain only one thing would've gotten taken care of in college, and that would not have been computer science.

Anyway, I've heard that behind every good man is a woman rolling her eyes. She probably has reason. After all, even a man cave needs a woman's touch. A writer years ago suggested one being from Mars and the other from Venus. Perhaps.

Getting back to class, our periods last an hour and 10 minutes here. During that time, there wasn't one second of dead air at the girls' table, not one. They were still discussing, in fact, as they walked out the door. Wars haven't been and won't be planned any better.

As for the boys, I heard maybe twenty words, and I prompted eight of them with my question. Same school, same event, familiar people.

My conclusion? God has a great sense of humor. While politicians lie, athletes perform, and the nightly news continuously gets delivered, the Man upstairs needs his well-deserved break. And since He'd already seen every episode of *That 70s Show*, *Seinfeld* and *The Big Bang Theory*, He came up with a great idea.

Every spring, he would send us all to prom.

The Humor in Loving Yourself

I read Louise Hay's book about how to love yourself – the premise is you're supposed to walk up to the mirror, look yourself in the eye and say, "I love you!" Quite frankly, this made me laugh, so hard I was told to get quiet by two of the Barnes & Noble employees. With my hand over my mouth, I continued to read.

I am not a touchy-feely type; the thought of looking myself in the mirror and saying anything seems…uncomfortable. Still, I love to read. And since I paid $16.95 for the book (not including my educator's discount!), I wasn't going to let my hard-earned money go to waste.

Moving forward, it was a Sunday and there was no one else in my condo to be found. Even the pet roach was dead. The cold winter got him and I found him toes up under my couch last Tuesday. The bathroom mirror is only steps away. I'd already seen this episode of *That 70s Show*, so there was no excuse…

Here I go. I am now standing in front of my mirror. I have successfully looked myself in the eye. There are way too many lines there, 'life scars' I call them, and I wasn't anything close to pretty. I take a deep breath and…what came out was, "You're a freak!" Oops, that's probably not what the author had in mind when she wrote her book, a bestseller by the way.

Still, I'm not going to quit after just one try. After all, even in tennis you get two serves before you lose the point. Here we go: "Did you get a free bowl of soup with that haircut? Is that a mullet? Didn't the 80s end 30-some years ago? What's up with that?" Okay, stop! Enough already.

You do get three strikes in baseball, though, right? Once more, here we go: "You know, your girlfriend is WAY better looking than you. How'd you pull that off anyway? I've heard about out punting your coverage, but your punter must've kicked the $#% out of that ball!"

Summary, this is difficult! Still, it got me thinking. Why are we so nice to other people yet we treat ourselves worse than trash? Or ask yourself this question: If you talked to other people the way you talk to yourself, exactly how many friends would you have? I can't speak for you, but my answer is a quick and simple ZERO!

I'm flawed and I'm beyond imperfect. But I'm not a quitter and I love psychological human experiments, and I couldn't care less if I'm the guinea pig. And, if I can't stare at me, I can at least tell me nicer things. So I tried it, for two weeks. Slowly at first, and then with some pace.

"You can do this! Put that Berry College degree to work, you're not dumb. Thank you. I love you. Well, maybe I don't love you, but you're getting better. If this were a sports banquet, at least you'd get the Most Improved Award."

Two weeks of this. Whenever my mind would go to #$#, I brought it back. "Thank you. I love you. You've got this. You deserve this. Come on! Hang in there. You're not so bad, pretty girlfriend, bad haircut and all. You deserve good things."

To summarize, here's what happens as you get better at this: Your life gets better. You attract people when they're at their best. It's almost like they're saying, "Hey, I like you, too. You're a nice guy! You DO deserve good things."

For you critics out there, look at it this way: It costs nothing. And I would be MORE than willing to bet, it's probably a heck-uva lot better than many of the thoughts that do run through your brain. No, I can't look in a mirror without laughing, that route isn't for me. I don't feel right, don't feel comfortable. (The book says, "That means you need more work!")

And I'm sure it does. After all, who am I to argue with Louise Hay? Still, since you're stuck with yourself, why not make the best of it? Why compliment others and then pound on yourself?

Anyway, I believe in this experiment. I won't quit. I'm not sure I love myself yet but, you know, I'm really not all that bad. And with my improving thoughts I'm enjoying a better life. It's called magic. Try it before you trash it...

Tune Out So You Can Tune In

I write this in full expectation of getting spayed and neutered by all the iPod people out there who "plug in" when they go for a run. I mean well, I do, and I hope your music is way better than all the sounds and conversations you're missing out on.

To be fair, I tried this once, and with a purpose. Wanting to break a certain barrier in the 5K, I timed the music where when *Only the Young* by Journey came on, I had exactly four minutes to be across that finish line. Not a second more.

On this day, Steve Perry sang his last note – I even pictured Louden Swain being hoisted atop wrestlers in the movie "Vision Quest" because the film ended with that song. Nope, not today, still had 100 meters to go. My music had started over; Mick Jagger was already rattling on about Mixed Emotions by the time I crossed.

Barrier remained unbroken. Experiment an utter failure. Earplugs pulled out in frustration.

Which brings me back to my bad attitude. In my marathon days, I ran with a girl who qualified for the Boston Marathon running under the midnight sun, though I still don't know where that took place. I met a New Yorker named Gerald Ford, nothing like our ex-president, who trained for the 26.2-mile race on a treadmill. I met a jovial African-American who nicknamed me "Peachtree Boy" when he found out I was from Atlanta. I met…well that's my point … I met people; formed friendships, had conversations that made my race, and perhaps my life a bit easier.

Fast forward to nowadays: I'm a social soul when I run. The sport has its pain, cramps, and suffering, but that's kind of the bond. When I come upon someone going my pace, I'll say hello. Often, they will take out their earphones, angrily look at me and growl, "What?"

Sorry, just trying to share the planet; to bond. I meant well, I promise. Unfortunately, it's very sad people like me are now an intrusion. Nothing more.

Makes me wonder why they put bells on bicycles these days. Who hears them? Does away with the courtesy of a runner or a biker announcing, "On your left" as they approach. Again, not heard. I've waved hello to great friends while passing – and never been seen.

I'd be remiss if I didn't mention the Peachtree Road Race as I write this, perhaps the most personality-filled 10K in the country. Pastors throw holy water on the participants, bands play, you meet people dressed in incredibly creative costumes, the crowd shouts at you from the sidelines.

Priceless! Call me crazy but I live for stuff like this. No offense to Journey, but Steve Perry can wait; I can pull that up on YouTube anytime I want. Besides, a little Journey goes great with a glass of cold beer. Trust me. I know this.

Anyway, if you're into the iPod thing, rock on, literally. I've proved controversial before when I boldly announced I don't always cheer for the underdogs. Bless you and your music, and bless you twice if your team beats someone it wasn't supposed to. I get it and I hear you, for what it's worth.

Still, I just left the river this morning, took my girlfriend there for the first time. A few of her comments jumped out at me.

"You can hear the river over there!" "Who were those people we just met; they seemed nice." "Wow, listen to the birds!"

It was peaceful; we stopped four times for conversations; solved all the world's problems except for the common cold and tennis elbow. While at it, we discussed laundry, full moons, Tom Petty and the sleep patterns of teenagers.

Yes, I heard all this and then some. And I'm a bit better than I used to be because of it.

A Piece of Me I'm Called to Share

I have a college friend who ran from Key West, Florida to Seattle, Wash., took him six months. When he finished, both the friend and the reporter in me couldn't wait to ask him one question: Why did he do it?

His answer remains one of my all-time favorites; "It was something to do." (My other favorite was when Stephen King was asked why he writes such gore; "What makes you think I have a choice?")

I think life is a lot about having something to do because, when there's nothing, you're forced to spend time with you and you. That, quite frankly, scares the hell out of some people. I know some people who can't even be quiet, they must fill the dead air with idle chit chat.

Eleven years ago, as I've written, I sat on an isolated bench in Juno Beach, Fla. with…nothing to do. A snapshot I'll always remember is one in my condo, with the furniture being taken off by my ex. I'm on the staircase and my dog, my beloved Jasper, ran up and sat right beside me. It's almost as if he were saying, "We don't have a pot to pee in, but I'm with you."

To this day – and my apologies to the macho out there – I can't look at a boy and his dog without getting a lump in my throat. The only love that rivals that comes from your mother.

For a year, I woke up on a couch, had very little to say, avoided people when I could, and constantly felt sorry for a self I pretty much despised. Through it all, I kept hearing in my head the words attributed to Buddhism, "Don't just do something, sit there!"

So, I did, constantly. Gratitude brought me back, and the fact that we are all ideas in the minds of God, and, unlike us, He doesn't make mistakes. Second, I read there's something we can do better than anybody else; something we're here to deliver. Personally, I still don't see what this knock-kneed, skinny brat from Madison, GA can do better than anyone else, but I was curious.

Third and finally, I was forced to do the scariest thing I've ever done, make peace with that face in the mirror. I had to go backwards. I mean, I'm not a murderer, I don't want to rob a bank today; I do wish people well, and I am jealous of literally no one.

The Man upstairs left me alone. It would be eight years before I'd be in a relationship, the one I'm in now. See how much work I had to do? Relationship attempts in the past would result in lost phone numbers, avoidance on one of the other's part, or perhaps I was working off an anti-GPS that would purposely keep me lost when searching for directions to meet up.

Present day, I think the end result is very simple but important. "The more you are able to like or love yourself, the more the whole world will follow suit." This is perhaps arrogant of me, but that is a very key line, underrated in its significance.

Back to present day: I'm at a school that played a large part in saving me, writing this even though it's a Sunday; even though it's spring break. I'm behind three locked doors, typing away in the library on a rainy day. Hear this – I have nothing to do until Tuesday, when I drive to St. Simons to see a friend. My girlfriend will be working; my friends are all busy. It's just me and me, and a silence I used to think was the loudest sound ever.

Eleven years ago, this would have me reaching for my anti-depressant, searching for somebody, anybody; anything to fill the void. Now, I sit isolated, until Tuesday.

And, though it took me 50-plus years to say this, I am filled with gratitude as I type these words: I'm looking forward to it.

God's love, self-love and love in general…

The Art of Getting Off Your Butt

So, this happened: I'm sitting in the library at my computer. Forgetting what I was doing and what I was writing, I just sat there, as if waiting on the monitor. I just stared at it. The machine matched my gaze. We both waited. The result: Nothing.

We're like that, we keep waiting. Even bringing God into the equation, it's the same point: You have to go first.

"Jump and the net will appear."

"When a web is begun, God sends thread."

"You don't have to see the whole staircase, just take the first step."

These are all, of course, well-known quotes. And I'm taking credit for none of them while trying to live them all.

We don't choose our dreams anyway – they choose us. And for a reason. Go the way you're wired. Use your gifts. Get started…

True it's easier said than done sometime, particularly after a fall. Why, I was so sad once, I slept for a year-and-a-half. When I awoke, I was living in Pennsylvania. How the hell did that happen? Still, I was trying and, if nothing else, survived it with stories to tell.

It's like this: Everybody needs something that sustains them; keeps them going; keeps the mind active. I can't help but recall the words of Paul "Bear" Bryant, legendary football coach at

Alabama. He was quoted as saying, "If I ever quit coaching football I'll die."

Eventually, he did quit. A month later, he died.

I'm a grateful soul because I have so much to write about. You may think you're boring but you're not. Ever raised a kid? Snuck a dollar out of your mom's purse? Kissed somebody you weren't supposed to? I can relate to missing the front end of a 1-and-1, losing the deciding match in tennis, and falling sick on Mile 11 of a marathon.

This is all good. After all, who wants to read about perfect man marrying perfect woman and their perfect life? NOBODY can relate. True mistakes, now that's where it's at!

In closing: Take up yoga. Lace em' up. Hit 'send.' Find a hobby or invent one. Fall through the roof of your school (oops, don't do that – not worth it!). Hear the naysayers and do it anyway.

Granted, perhaps this is now easy for me to say. I'm fortunate to be coming from a good place, respectfully knowing all this could change.

Still, I'll finish and send this off to my girlfriend; may be a bit nervous about it. Will she like it? Will anybody? Still I smile - there was a time when I gave up on even having a girlfriend. You know why I have one? I called her. Didn't really know what to expect, but I did it.

It was, after all, a start...

Instruction Book for Graduates and Life in General

With apologies to H. Jackson Browne

* Have cliques but don't be afraid to socialize outside of them.

* If you can't decide, flip a coin. When the coin is in the air, you'll know what to do.

* When a good friend asks for advice, be honest even if it hurts. In the end, they will appreciate the advice and you.

* Be true to yourself. This can be harder than you think.

* Keep a journal. Reading it will be priceless as time goes by.

* Don't force things, friendships or relationships. Whatever or whoever is supposed to be in your life will be.

* A simple life philosophy: Love as much as you can and give thanks at every turn.

* Remember the words of MLK: "Take the first step in faith. You don't have to see the whole staircase, just take the first step!"

* Be aware of your weaknesses, but make sure you work on your strengths! After all, your strengths are what you will use to make your living.

* When spotting someone you find attractive, approach with confidence or don't approach at all.

* When stressed, take a 30-minute run or workout break. It can reset your mind and change the dynamics of your day.

* Be grateful! The fact that you had the luxury to shower this morning makes you one of the luckiest people on the planet.

* Don't sweat it if you don't have your major or your life planned already. Good things evolve over time. Trust, and enjoy, the journey!

* Keep a list of things that make you feel good. Refer to it during tough times.

* Regarding money - save when you can, be generous when you can, and if you owe it, pay it.

* When in doubt, simply be nice. If this is too hard, walk away.

* "Be kind whenever possible. It is always possible." – Dalai Lama

* Be the kind of person you'd like to hang out with.

* Goals are fine, but only if you enjoy each step of the way.

* Remember: God has your back and there ARE good people in this world.

* Call your mom. It will make her day.

* Learn someone's name and call them by it. People like to feel included, knowing who they are is a very important first step.

* Avoid clutter. There's a reason you feel better after cleaning your closet, trunk, or room. It's mental as well as physical!

* A bumper sticker I read: "Be yourself, the world will adjust." That's a tad mind blowing but I like the sound of it.

* Find a good study or support group.

* Find or create your "physical haven." It could be a library, your dorm room, or your favorite coffee shop. Go there whenever possible.

* Get to know your teachers. Don't just be in the class for a grade.

* Go to a college football game. The energy is boundless.

* Remember: blaming is the easy way out. At the end of the day, you're 100% responsible for your life and your decisions. Make good ones!

* Be on time or even early if possible.

* If you find you must edit yourself to remain in a relationship, then it's not the relationship for you.

* When in doubt, keep it simple! Life is complicated enough.

* Have a routine, but don't be afraid to break it every now and then.

* Work hard when you have to but take the time off when you get to.

* Peace, good luck and don't forget to go back home and visit!

Youer Than You

I just read this sentence, written by Shannon Kaiser, that kind of blew me away. It said, "The more you you show, the better your life will flow."

My mind went to all our quirks and how so many people try to extinguish them. This sentence made me happy, it means I can have a sensible, sane, rational conversation in the corner of Dunkin Donuts, complete with gesturing, with only myself. And it's okay...

Some quirks:

- My girlfriend can't swim in a straight line.
- My oldest brother would get lost on a track.
- My college friend would never put his wallet, keys, and ID in the same place. We'd have to search three times over the entire room before we could go to the dining hall.
- Sheldon Cooper must knock on the door three times. (Okay, it's only a TV show, but you know people like that, right?)
- My friend Phil almost pukes when he's around ketchup.
- When I hear Fleetwood Mac, I think it's a sign from God. Also, my boxer shorts must be blue, buying packs with assorted colors is not an option.

I'm recalling the words of one of our greatest poets of all time

– Dr. Seuss. "Today you are you, that is truer than true. No one can be more youer than you."

People are drawn to passion, genuineness, being real. Social media, unfortunately, makes us compare, makes us feel not up to par, like maybe we're losing at some game we're not sure how to play; not even sure when or if we signed up for it.

If you're editing yourself at your job or around your friends, then you're at the wrong job; around the wrong people. Sameness is boring; like canned speeches or monotone lectures.

Anyway, while writing this, a colleague just walked by, saw me talking out this essay. He knows me; he just smiled and shook his head. This used to bug me, though it reminds me of a true story – one about the lady who almost called the police on me because I was talking to myself on the porch at my watering hole last summer.

Call them. Arrest me. Sue me. All I know is this:

Today, it's Friday; I have on my lucky boxers. I'm talking to myself in a library, near no one.

I have essays to write; words to get down on paper. This is, to me, way more important than small talk about the weather; or me pretending to give a damn about an NBA game. My mind goes to Gone with the Wind regarding small talk: *Frankly my dear…*

So, in signing off, I will attempt to copy the good Dr. Seuss:
"Do with me what you will; I have my quirks to fulfill."
Cheers to you being you!

The Art of Saying Yes

There's nothing worse, in little kid world, than when your best girl gives you your dog tag back and tells you she's leaving you because you have the cooties. All this shortly after you've dropped an easy pop fly to lose your Little League game a mere three days before.

There I was, broken by life and disheartened at the age of 10, nowhere to go, nobody to love, and not a soul in sight I could copy the history homework from. Momma told me there'd be days like this. As usual, however, I failed to listen.

There's just not too much worse than being sad. It's a disconnected feeling. People pass you in the hall as if you're not even there; you're the last one picked for kickball and you don't even feel you can offer up a prayer because God must be WAY too busy for little old you. So, you sit and you mope and you don't even hear when the teacher calls on you in class to read page 42, paragraph five. The other kids laugh because you've been nailed – the joke is once again on you and you alone. The laughter hurts, it passes your heart and goes straight to your soul.

There's a story out there, and I'm not sure who I'm stealing it from, about a priest who's always, and I mean all-ways happy. If it's raining, he's laughing. If his shoestring pops, he's laughing. If the news is bad, he's at worst – smiling. He's the kind of guy who probably smiled at the girl in fifth grade when she gave him his dog tag back. Frankly, sometimes this kind of people like this makes you sick, but let's move on.

"What's your secret?" a man asked. "Why are you always so (bleeping) happy! Do you have any clue what's going on in the world right now?" Cynics always want to ask this; as if each segment of the news is supposed to bring you just a little more down – and sad – and bad – and mad. They depend on this for their own sanity; they need that misery-loves-company thing like a kid needs their morning cartoons.

"It's easy," the man replied. "I simply say yes to life and all that it offers."

I had to think when I first read this one. I know I didn't say yes to the above rejection episode. Am quite sure, if I'd written the script, I would've caught that pop fly on that Madison, Georgia summer night. I know I wouldn't have walked out on the Homecoming Court as the queen's escort with my fly open in front of everyone. (And for the record, the girl I escorted didn't say yes to that either!). I don't remember saying yes when I watched my dad die of cancer; nor when dear old mom went to join him two summers ago.

I think it all depends on your belief of life after death. If you think this is it – you enjoy your share of *Big Bang Theory* episodes, try to get out of jury duty, advance through prom, college, career, and family and then boom – game over, then okay. That'd would make that yes thing hard though, right?

Still it got me thinking. What if the old priest was on to something? What if my ex-wife was right when she told me to get out? What if Jolene Hensler was supposed to tell me to get lost when I tried to explain the above fly-open incident? What if the Christians, the Buddhists, and the Episcopalians all know what they're talking about?

Okay, so hindsight is twenty-twenty. Perhaps that makes the point of all this not to wait for the hindsight. I had to sit down when that thought worked its way past my TV dinners and stale pizzas and found its way into my skull. What if it all works out? If it's not okay in the end, then it's simply not the end. Really?

I read once where God was like a GPS. If you make a wrong turn, He doesn't berate you and call you an idiot. He simply tells you where to go now – from here. When you make the next wrong move, He simply recalculates. There's a glow inside when I think of it this way.

Everything is going to be all right. Does this mean I can afford to just relax and enjoy all of this? What if I lose the big race, get rejected again and lose some more loved ones? What if there's another President election and I must read all that crap on Facebook about everyone's sacred opinion? What if my beloved cross country team doesn't do well at state and my top girl transfers.

I smile a lot more now in my older age. The saddest things that have ever happened to me have all worked out better than I could've planned. Yes, even my parent's deaths – I feel closer to my dad and mom now than I ever have – and if that doesn't make any sense then call me weird. My divorce – an event that threw me into a clinical depression – has worked out well for us both.

It all leads to where you are now. I got up today and went to school – Prom Weekend no less – and felt the buzz and the excitement that only a bunch of hyped up teenagers can generate. At a track meet Tuesday, I had a junior come up to me with a smile so big I could see her gums. Do you know what she told me? "My mother thinks I'm awesome!" I cried I laughed so hard – it was such a cute, raw, random, from-the-heart-statement.

I've learned to think her awesome, too – and all of this as well. I don't know what happened before I came here – not sure what's going to happen when I go. In retrospect - because I'm still getting the lesson not to rely on hindsight - is that I wouldn't trade it for anything. Life isn't something that owes you – and people with that attitude do NOT make me smile or laugh or say yes. In fact, that philosophy makes me want to pick up that fly ball I dropped and perhaps deposit it somewhere.

As I said, it's Prom Weekend here. Our junior and senior girls have emptied out into Atlanta for hair appointments, last minute preparations on their dresses, all that. The guys – trying to be cool – will wait till the last minute. One guy asked his date out in front of everyone at assembly. Another took care of it at chapel. I remember a story once about a guy – I won't mention any names but his initials are Richard Pickering - who put his wife-to-be up on a parasail. When she was in the air, he wrote in the sand, "Will you marry me?" When she landed, he handed her a glass of champagne and the ring.

See? There are so many good stories out there! We did nothing to earn this! I can only think back to my early days when she said "No!" All good. I laugh at this now; I'm not that old man yet but damn it, I'm learning.

In present day, I've already read my directions on my GPS and understand my role completely. My job is to move forward – to love as much as possible and to give thanks at every single turn. This makes me smile; laugh out loud even. In fact, I couldn't be happier.

And to think, I don't even have a date for the prom…

A 'Please Read Plea' to our Hallways

Sometimes it takes so little, something as small as getting our head out of own dramas and reaching out. It's not complicated – just a hello, how's your day, what's going on with you? It's just about showing that, quite simply, you give a damn. If you don't, well maybe that's part of the problem.

There is a BRILLIANT school teacher out West who makes students vote on their peers for "Student of the Week." Truly, she couldn't care less who it is, she's just looking for patterns. Who never gets voted for? Who never votes? She's been doing it since Columbine. After all, it's the isolated people who walk the halls and shoot people. The rejects, the outcasts, the people who think they don't matter. They are the ones crying for help, crying for love.

I applaud this teacher and she is now my hero. I'm grateful to God for my very own life, because I get to walk the halls where I work and reach out. Yes, I'm flawed. Often I'm preoccupied about some self-inflicted drama and I simply walk past. Thanks to my new hero, I now know this is no longer acceptable.

Like I said, it takes so little. Learn people's names. Catch them doing something right. Give them a smile. We're all in this together. This Earth trip, in my simple opinion, is supposed to be celebrated, enjoyed, cherished. It should be about making memories and posting fun stuff on Instagram or Facebook. Laughing in the halls about the latest adventure. Cheering or pouting over your sports teams.

As for today, I'm going to stand at a track meet in the rain. Rumor may have it, with my tennis background, I'm not the greatest track coach that ever put on the spikes. Sometimes people ask me things I don't know the answer to. Often I want to give them the right advice but I'm not sure what it is. It frustrates me, eats at me when I try to sleep.

But you know...I can always give a damn, no matter what I know or don't know. I can always smile. If nothing else, I can simply be there for them.

Yes, I can always do that....

And peace, always peace!

The Joy of Participating

"If you don't think this is a good day, then try missing one of them!" That quote came from the late Zig Ziglar, a former author and motivational speaker who used to set the world on fire with his talks. This line resonated within me and was reinforced this past week.

You see, I did miss one of them, a day that is, due to an illness. I was ordered by our school nurse to get some rest, drink fluids, you know the drill. On Wednesday, I complied and for the first time in my 13-year history at my work, school came and went without me.

My ego rebelled. Who's going to open the library? What about carpool? Who's going to sub for Alice? What about track practice and carpool again? I made myself important in my head while I lay in bed for the next 36 hours. How, after all, could a school day possibly go by without me?

Well, it did. And everything got handled just fine, me and my ego be damned. It got me thinking about a confrontation between a boss and an employee years ago, when the employee stressed his self-importance while the boss simply pointed to a stack of about 78 resumes sitting on his desk. "You see that stack?" he asked. "That's just SOME of the people who want your job. Now get out of here!" Off the employer went, or so I was told.

Now healthy, my brain made sense of all this, or the best my brain can do anyway. I figure there are three rules when it comes to settling down, and no, they are NOT location, location, location. They are location, chemistry and timing, with the order varying by the situation.

Once you've got that down, there are three rules to finding work. They are as follows, and please note these are in order:

1. Do what you love;
2. Do what you love; and last and most important...
3. Do what you love.

By trial and error and perhaps because the angels of heaven got tired of watching me flounder, I have the do what you love thing down. Don't get me wrong, I've flipped burgers at McDonalds, sold pots and pans door to door, was disguised as a banker for three years, worked every multi-level marketing scheme known to man, and fed tennis balls out of a basket for more years than I care to remember.

Which brings me to my conclusion: I want to participate, period. I don't want to miss another day. A former girlfriend used to tell me that I would NEVER miss a college party because I was afraid I'd miss something. She was right, damn right. I hated my sick day. Things happened, kids flirted, lockers slammed, coaches coached, teachers taught. I missed it. Missed every bit of it.

Sure, the school will go on long after I'm gone. My job is to give it what I've got while I'm there. Thank you, Mr., Ziglar. Thank you for your words of wisdom and may you rest in peace. Me, I'm tired of resting.

I've got to get back to work.

Carpool Zen 101

If you can find spirituality working carpool you can find it anywhere. My goal is to make it such a Zen experience that one day I'll walk inside feeling as if I've slept for eight hours. I almost got hit by a Ford Explorer two weeks ago, almost slept lots longer than that.

It's a process that began in anger. I don't get mad much – save when my favorite football team does that delayed draw thing on 3rd-and-1. (Why you want to make a runner gain six yards just to gain one will forever elude me, but I'm at peace with that. I think.)

Anyway, carpool equals adventure. I've seen a Honda Civic almost take out the entire Pagano family, bear hugged Georgia Symbas and saved her life, and nicely told a mom it's not proper to hold up the line simply because she's texting. I'll withhold her name to protect the guilty.

It's a challenge because I'm the first person people see in the morning. I start their day, if I do it badly because I'm not at my best, the ripple effect can spread to Texas before morning break. No, that's not just a cute line, that's a fact. It's not about us, but we are hugely important all the same.

It's not what you do, it's how you do it. I've learned this. I've seen whistling garbage men, encouraging taxi drivers, and joyous dishwashers. Unfortunately, I've also seen pampered, ticked-off ballplayers, wealthy nitpickers and people spreading anger simply because that's all they've got within.

At carpool, Gracie brought me coffee for two years. Sophie gave me her last chicken biscuit. A mom gave me some hot chocolate just to keep my hands warm. Yes, I work at that kind of place, an oasis if there ever was one. Still, I have learned, and who would've thought it would be carpool where I did?

Today the sun shined on my shoulders as Ashley Whitehead greeted me with her standard, "What's up, Dunn?" A parent rolled down her window to ask if I'd read any good books lately. Another one asked what my next blog would be about. Dr. Swann, as he always does, told me he appreciated me getting him across.

I've learned to love it out here even when it's cold. I get paid to spread positive energy. Period. It's a challenge, but I get to be the start of smiles every morning. (Take that, Texas!) Dad always taught me to leave em laughing. Mom always made me be nice. I know every morning that, if I can get through carpool doing both, the rest of my day should be cinch.

Anyway, the bell just rang, I must go. Taking off my vest, I'm realizing that I don't feel like I've slept for eight hours. But you know, I'm not ticked off, either. In fact, I feel pretty bleeping good.

And I'm grateful to carpool for teaching me all this...

One Magical Fact

If you talked to other people the way you talk to yourself, how many times a day would you get beaten up? How many detentions would you get? How many teams would you get thrown off? We laugh at this. But still, it's perhaps the most important problem that needs solving.

Before we go any further: No, I am not a doctor, a psychologist, a psychiatrist, or a counselor. I have better qualifications. You see, I am a sub. Not sure what I know, but I hear things. Boy, do I hear things. Like this: Yes, I made a D on that test because I am a dingbat. Or from back in my tennis coaching days, "That was the worst shot, ever!" I wanted to interject right there and say. Really? THAT was the worst shot ever?

Based on these wonderful examples of self-talk and my own experiences, I have come to this conclusion: Without a positive relationship with your own self, even reading self-help books and hearing inspirational lectures can be almost meaningless. It's almost like you're wanting a cool breeze on a hot summers night, but you've got the windows closed. Without self-love, the information has nowhere to go, you're blocking it. It goes somewhere else!

I see the paradox here. We're taught to love others. Not ourselves. Often we overcompensate. We look outward, ignore our own needs. Meanwhile, God patiently waits…

And this bothered me, followed me past carpool, into the class room and off to practice. How do you treat yourself? Maybe it's time you think about what you're thinking about. Let me give you a personal sample: It's October as I write this; it's cross country season – we're running at the Chattahoochee river. I love to flatter myself and tell people I run with the kids, but actually I'm in the back, way back there, with Coach Lewis and Coach Jones.

My brain kicks in. "Man, you used to run with the top guys, and now you are behind the JV runners! What is wrong with you? Why are you so slow? What happened?" I stopped myself right then and addressed my thoughts. What if I talked to my runners that way?

I pictured it: I'm at the finish line at the Asics Invitational – yellow note pad in hand. I'm waiting on my last runners – waiting and waiting and waiting. They finish and I approach. "Wow," I say, "you're really good kids but MAN you people are slow! Seriously, 28:42, I know this, I just timed you. What's up with that?"

This would be undoing all the great that Coach Jayaraj is doing with our teams. This could or should get me slapped and fired. This, and thank goodness I thought this, is no longer acceptable!

Off to work I went. I found one of my books which was something about mirror work. It said to look yourself in the mirror and say, "I love you." I can't do it. I tried. Every time I look at myself in the mirror I start laughing. Or at best, it goes something like this: Really? You're going to go out looking like…that! Did you get a free bowl of soup with that haircut?

See the problem? With the law of attraction, the loving energy of God can only connect with your own loving energy. Love equals love – otherwise off it goes. I realize you guys may be a little young for the law of attraction, but I'm trying to save you

40 years! And man, I'm getting old! And that's why I don't look in the mirror! Jayaraj always says the clock doesn't lie. Neither does the mirror.

Let's move on. I figured that if I can't love me, I can love God; we'll start there. So, while at carpool, I often look up and simply say, "Thank you." And I promise if you can say it there, you can say it anywhere. Little things. We're at the starting line and Jackie Addy remembered to put on her bib number. Thank you. It's 20 degrees and Liam Hill remembered to put on sweat pants. Thank you. You start with gratitude; you work your way up.

Step two: Go to, at least self-acceptance. The students at my school are wonderful. In my 14 years of walking the halls, they continue to make my day – they've almost never ruined it. In fact, I live for the randomness that is the teenage mind.

Seniors make my every morning because my office is right by the Senior Commons. I can hear everything they say. I wish I could write stuff like that! Even in running, I'm getting it down: I'll leave it to Jayaraj to make them faster. My job – where I am now – is to like me and love my runners, and I don't care how slow they are! I'll stand at the finish line for 38:42, I don't care! And if I get mad, I'll simply look up and utter, "Thank you, thank you, thank you."

In moving on, let's get presumptuous here. See yourself through God's eyes. He's just given you the gift of life, a gift you've done nothing to deserve. He's given you your uniqueness, your talents, your passions, again, that you've done nothing to deserve. He's given you this love, instilled you with greatness to boot and...your response? "But I'm an idiot! I run slow! I made a 42 on my test."

Right there, you're putting yourself at odds with the whole universe! You're closing that window people. It's all about opening that window, perhaps a crack at first, then a bit more. God is for you; the world is for you. Now YOU must be for you. It works from the inside out, NOT the other way around!

I'll close with one sentence, and this is $22,528 worth of self-help books in one fell swoop: **The more comfortable you get with yourself – the more you're able to like or love yourself, the more the whole world will follow suit. I repeat: The more comfortable you get with yourself – the more you're able to like or love yourself, the more the whole world will follow suit.**

That is magical… and that is fact.

Thank you.

The Art of Doing What You Love

At the watering hole. A Wednesday night. Lost in thought. Shuffling Senior Night in sports, Springfest activities, Prom Week, and writing stories inside my head.

"Are you happy?" The voice came from my left; jarred me alert. It was a man and his son, enjoying dinner and a drink. "Are you happy?" he repeated. "You look tired."

"Yes, I'm fortunate to be happy," I managed. "Was at a track meet all day yesterday; going back tomorrow." With that I returned to my thoughts.

"You know," he continued, "people say beauty is skin deep. I don't think so. I think happy people are beautiful people. It's the happy people we're drawn to." He stared at me; his eyes curious as to my response.

So, he wouldn't think me comatose, I did answer. "Yes, I do think happy people have a glow about them; sort of an attractor factor if you will." With that I went back to my school week, writing my story inside my head. It was going okay, but I needed a connecting paragraph.

"You know, people always talk about finding their passion," he went on. "It's really quite easy." This got my attention – it's a hot topic with, well, pretty much everybody. "Go on," I prodded.

"What would you do for free? That's all you have to ask yourself. Whatever that is, that's what you should do for a living."

My mind went to recall: I traced back my history. I taught tennis until the very thought of it pained me in my stomach and rose to the top of my chest. Was disguised as a banker for three years and fooled no one. Tried my hand at sales, mostly in multilevel marketing schemes. My bosses were very underwhelmed and wished me luck …anywhere else.

One day I went back to my roots and reconnected with sportswriting. While headed to the gym I passed through a hallway. Kids were at their lockers; standing around, talking, flirting. Remembering my sweet mom's love for the school and her passion for the kids, the hairs stood up on my arms. I got a little choked up.

Eventually the kids left the hall. I did not.

"Come again Friday," the man said. "Bring your girlfriend. We'll talk some more."

He and his son got up and I must say I had to get a look at this guy. He had a foreign accent, I knew that much. He was a tad overweight, but I'm not judging. Even as a writer, I'm not good at describing people, words always escape me when I try to go into this mode.

Maybe I'll just describe him as beautiful. Yeah, that's it, he was beautiful.

What Do You Believe In?

Susan Sarandon asked this question in *Bull Durham*. Today, I'm bored so I'm going to answer it. Besides, what you believe is what you get; for what it's worth, this is what I've got.

I believe if you sing a Peaches and Herb song out loud at your watering hole, there's a pretty decent chance you'll get beaten up.

I believe if you want to see peace, look at a mother's face when she's talking about her kid.

I believe in hot bowls of chili, though I'm not sure if they're good for you or not.

I believe sales people would have more success dressed in t-shirts and jeans. It's less threatening, therefore your guard is down.

I believe in staying far away from special nights for the high school kids. I don't want to see what they're doing because I remember the things I did.

I believe the only constant is change – though that's often hard to accept.

I believe in naps on couches, because naps and couches are two great things.

I believe school teachers get picked for jury duty a lot.

I believe in sitting quietly in a room alone – and enjoying it.

I believe I've never met a Midwesterner I didn't like.

I believe people should have to take a Breathalyzer before getting on social media.

I believe in getting rid of things you no longer need, which includes people in many cases.

I believe the National Anthem should be played, rarely sung.

I believe college football should get rid of the Blue-Gray game.

I believe in doing away with hair products that keep your hair from going gray. Aging naturally is a badge of honor – fighting it only increases its speed.

I believe in meditation even though I'm beyond horrible at it.

I believe in opening doors for women, and saying yes sir and yes ma'am. Unfortunately, this often puts me in the minority.

I believe in complimenting people on their shoes whether I like them or not. It often leads to interesting conversations.

I believe in running without iPods. I want to talk to people and hear the natural noises.

I believe in hugs, high-fives and smiles. I want people to know I come in peace.

I believe Dunkin Donuts will always have the best coffee, new chains be damned.

I believe getting sick is a blessing in disguise. It's God's way of telling you to slow down.

I believe women look better with less makeup.

I believe the written word is a contract with God, and I've learned to thank the heavens in advance on yellow notecards.

I believe in keeping a "gloat" file in my email box. Whenever I'm down, I pull it out and read.

I believe there's no such thing as a good seat for a meeting.

I believe in chicken tenders day at my school, and making sure I get to the front of the line before the kids do.

I believe in class reunions only as I've gotten older, mainly because no one cares what anyone does or did for a living anymore.

I believe there really is such thing as a stupid question.

I believe having nothing to do causes panic in younger years; it's a reason for celebration in older ones.

I believe in my mother's iced tea. Everyone else's is in a tie for second.

And finally, I believe in getting to the point. With that said, I will now shut up.

Who's Favored...or Does It Matter?

I've always been confused regarding this underdog vs. favorites thing. Don't get me wrong, I enjoyed watching Rudy make his tackle before the closing credits. Got a lump in my throat when the small-town basketball team from Indiana got it done in *Hoosiers*. And Rocky, he put up one helluva fight, though I still think he should've left Adrian alone until after he'd taken a shower.

Anyway, this is what happened: In my athletic years, I was at one of our sports banquets. An athlete had just finished an undefeated season in her sport. I won't mention her name because, quite frankly, I don't remember it. Anyway, when it got to the MVP award, there was no speech from the coach. It was simply, "And the MVP of course is...." And off the student went to get her trophy.

My brain, normally a dormant thing during those years, went to work. Why would the best player warrant the shortest speech? Why wasn't her trophy perhaps bigger since she was the best? Why did it seem like everyone took her for granted?

Sometimes, quite frankly, people do take the best player for granted. The hallway conversations are often, "I know she won, but how'd everyone else do?" Also, and often, the only time the favorite's names comes up is when she loses. A win is already counted on, marked off in the scorebook. "She lost? Really?"

It's almost as if it were a sin for her to be human.

I coach running these days, some toe the starting line simply hoping to get it over with so they can go to the lake. Others just want to beat that kid two rows over. Some really go for it, and I've learned through my past to applaud and love these humans.

Years ago, I loved watching my top gun – Ben Davies – break the tape race after race. I watched him train; knew what he put himself through. Also, not having a girl who could compete with her, I silently marveled and pulled for Lovett's Serena Tripodi when she won her state crowns.

They were favored. They won. Didn't bother me then; doesn't bother me now.

It's automatic with most: When two teams play they naturally pick the underdog. I'm a small-town boy who used to play tennis, I often lived the role as the underdog. Still, being from that small town often cast me as the favorite, and I knew I'd worked hard as well. Was my fire fueled any different either way?

It's funny now: The cross country team I coach has a shot at being preseason ranked #1 in the state come fall. Now, the targets will be on our own precious backs. Worms turn, roles reverse, life happens.

I guess it is and always will be situational. Still, I'm going to go out on a limb here and tell you that come next cross country season, I'm going to go against the grain. I'm going to root for the favorites. And now that I think of it: Whether they win or lose, favored or not, I'll probably get a lump in my throat either way...

They Say It's Your Birthday

I have a birthday coming up and it got me to thinking…how the concept has changed, that is.

I remember being 5 or so, when a day lasted for a week, or at least that's what you crammed into it. You sprang out of bed, blew out your candles, threw some cake at your brothers. Your mom made you pose for "The Birthday Picture." Dad rolled his eyes.

Mom took the film to the pharmacy and waited the obligatory week for the pics to come back, while you were off, playing kick the can, hide and seek, monopoly, baseball games in the yard, dirt clod battles, because you could hurl those at other kids and not end up in law suits back then.

I still remember Paul Reid pegging me in the back of the head with the largest clump of dirt ever resting on Madison, Ga. soil. Made me cry. I got him back by saying something bad about Led Zeppelin. We shook hands, called it even. We're friends to this very day.

You went to bed at 9 p.m. because those were the house rules. You put on your pajamas – complete with the feet already in them. You pretended to brush your teeth, and off to bed you went. Parents planned 12 hours' worth of energy in your day, but God gave you 16. It was a Mars/Venus thing though that book wouldn't be out for years, and that was about the sexes.

Birthday – your day – though I still remember screwing it up even back then. One year Mom said I could invite eight friends over; I asked nine. My heart dropped even then when I had to tell one he couldn't come over. Len McElhannon, if you're out there, please accept my apologies 53 years later.

Now, to present day, I often wonder what happened to the days when it took a year for a year to go by (to quote from Sam Hutcheson), and how May got here so fast when I just put up my Christmas tree.

The thought of jumping out of bed ended somewhere around the time the Beatles broke up. Now, it's a matter of calling roll of my body parts. Head? Mattress marks still on it. Neck? Sore, but trying to lift. Back? Hurts like (bleep). Legs? Stiff! Ready to get up? Lord no! (Hit snooze button).

I think back to when getting my "birthday" physical was a mere inconvenience, something I did while making other plans. Now, it makes me reach for a drink, but wait, I can't. That could throw off my innards and my X-rays and my liver readings. And isn't there cancer in my family? And weren't my PSA levels up last year? Does wine help or hurt that?

Still, it's May. Winter finally left, though it didn't seem happy about it. In my brain, there is still youth. I want to ride off with my Holy Innocents' seniors on their upcoming graduation trip; take in a Braves game; cart my pretty girlfriend out West, or was it South? Hike the Appalachian Trail backwards, just because. I want to do things in general, because that's what I came down here for.

Problem is, I'm not sure all my body parts will cooperate.

Oh, well, Happy Birthday to me, I guess…

Ode to a Retiring Police Officer

I'm walking into Dunkin Donuts at 5:30 this morning, three cops are sitting in the corner. Of the trio, one is sticking out profusely on this day. Looking at his police garb – the gun, holster, badge, and the like – it is his smile that is leaning across the table.

After 20-plus years on the force, 12 of them in Atlanta, today is his last day. By sharing a corner of the coffee shop, I've come to know this man over the years, though not by name. I still don't know his nor he mine. If memory serves, he's not even from this country, though he's spent most of his life defending it.

I shake his hand with as big a smile as I've got at this early hour, though it was his partner, Officer Tom, who kept things going. "Tell him what you're going to do now," he said.

The soon-to-be-retiree smiled even bigger, if possible, and then began. "We've sold our house and our stuff; we've bought an RV and we're going to travel across the country. We're going to start up in Michigan, work for fourth months at a campground, and then head southwest. From there, we'll simply follow the warm weather."

I got goosebumps, I really did. Besides, who deserves a great retirement more than a police officer or a veteran? And maybe I'm subconsciously stealing from Steinbeck here in "Travels with

Charley" but how many of you can hear this roaming-the-countryside thing without wanting to get in the car and go?

The thoughts of taking in a backwoods coffee shop somewhere between Kentucky and Arkansas and people-watching. Or going to a minor-league baseball game in Lancaster, PA just because. Catching the fireworks in Denver on the 4th of July. Go for a run somewhere in Oregon – and not give a rip about time, distance, or pace.

There's a part of us all that wants to go, I think. "There are two sides to this," the officer went on. "There are people that respond the way you did, the people who want to go, and there are the ones who tell you you're crazy. Still, I think even those people want to do it. Problem is, most people don't have the guts."

Reflecting over my coffee, I'm thinking of what it means to be a cop in a big city these days - in a world where snipers stand above and take pot shots at concert-goers. Where a kid can't get his physics book out of his locker without, sometimes literally, dodging bullets. Days where turning on the news requires holding your breath, crossing your fingers, praying to God.

I'm running now at the river. It's early again, the deer aren't even up. Am thinking of freedom, how I can feel it now to my right in the sight and sounds of this river. Am seeing this man filling up with gas somewhere in Bradfield, if that place even exists. Taking a walk besides a cornfield in Topeka. Oversleeping in Bakersfield.

I can't help but smile as I finish my run and stretch on the picnic table; and only one thought enters my head: Happy Trails.

And I've rarely, if ever, meant that more in my life.

Me Wars

Me, 1970s: I can't believe it! They've passed a law where you can't ride in the back of trucks anymore! I ride in the back of my coach's all the time – I just jump out when I get home.

Me, now: You can't even put students INSIDE your car now. Legal reasons.

1970s: What are legal reasons?

Now: If someone is bored, they can sue you for something. It all falls under the umbrella of "legal reasons."

1970s: Do you sue people?

Now: No, I go home, punch my pillow until I'm exhausted, then go to my watering hole and forget about it. If I'm owed something, society will pay me one way or the other – it works the other way, too.

1970s: Sometimes I think this world is going nuts. How is it where you are?

Now: It's batcrap crazy! You can get shot at almost anywhere, anyplace, anytime and people are still raising hell about an election that happened two years ago. Love him or hate him, everyone knows he should never go on Twitter!

1970s: Who's Twitter?

Now: It's a thing not a person - something people get themselves in trouble on, perhaps no one more than our very own president.

1970s: Yes, times are crazy. Ronald Reagan is running for President now, an actor! How crazy is that?

Now: Just wait…oh, just you wait…

1970s: Did I fulfill my dream? Am I playing in the NBA?

Now: Even the NBA players aren't playing in the NBA. They mope around until postseason; then spend some parts of the fourth quarter hustling. As for you, no! You're small, skinny, you can't jump and besides – you can't even SEE from as far out as you used to shoot!

1970s: Can you believe the money they make? One of the NFL quarterbacks is making $90,000 a year!

Now: Ha! We had a boxer years ago – Mike Tyson - that spent more than that on pigeons – and I'm not kidding.

1970s: Well, do our sports teams ever win championships?

Now: I'm not sure that's legal in Georgia; I'll get back to you on that one. We are REALLY good at getting REALLY close, though.

1970s: Do I get the girl?

Now: You do, and then you don't, and then you do again.

1970s: Is something wrong with me?

Now: Oh, you're a complete wack job! But you care and you love a lot. You have learned that's all that matters, people love that. And it helps them overlook your wack-job-edness.

1970s: Where do I live? And why?

Now: You live at a school – you have a library, a computer and books. When you get bored, you write essays and put them on this thing called Facebook. You do it for no other reason than you want to – it seems like an honest, fun-though-perhaps-vulnerable thing to do.

1970s: What's a Facebook?

Now: It's something as beautiful as finding your old girl-friend, as boring as reading about a recipe or a workout, as angry as a political rant, and as pretty as a picture. It's a perfect place for me to exercise my attention deficit disorder.

1970s: Attention deficit disorder?

Now: It's something we all need to take in the massive info; yet something diagnosed where people can make money curing it. It's a crazy loop. Money, as usual, is involved.

1970s: Do you have all these things – Facebook? Twitter? Attention deficit?

Now: I must have the first two because of work; as for medical – I've been diagnosed from everything to depressed, to poor attention span to Tourette's Syndrome (don't ask). The key is to decompress, spend time alone, get to know the God you believe in, work hard at being your own self in a world that won't let you. Read. Write. Run.

70s: Sounds like you've become a weirdo!

Now: And then some. But I'm me and I'm happy, two not-so-easy things to accomplish! I must go now – a kid needs help with her essay. The fact she asked me just made my day.

70s: I've got to go. You're boring me and I'm not real sure I can handle all this! Besides, *Columbo* and *McMillan & Wife* are coming on. I'll look you up when I get to the future.

Now: Sounds great. Friend me on Facebook – follow me on twitter.

70s: Good grief!

Now: That's exactly what it can lead to, my man... You're catching on already...

Meditations From a Shrink's Office in West Palm

Things are great now, but this is my tribute to when they weren't. Twelve years later, I still don't know how to give proper thanks. After all, if my math is correct, Dr. Rosen is now somewhere between 96 and 108 years old. How do I repay him? What can I do? What to say?

One day a month, and paying out of my own shallow pockets that were collecting no money and nothing but laundry lent, I went to see Dr. Rosen for counseling. Personally, I think we all need it at one time or another; I knew damn well I did.

For the record, it's not like on TV. I never stretched out on a couch; was never hypnotized, nor was I judged because of my birth order or fixations on mothers or fathers or tree stumps. It was useful, so useful that in present day I can still hear his voice, his probing questions, can still see his eyes peering over those thick, dark glasses.

How's your esteem? How are your thoughts? Are you moving forward, doing something every day to get yourself closer to what you want to become? Do you have something to do, something to love, something to look forward to?

Turned out, it was his last year on the job – I fear I drove him into retirement. He got his money's worth out of me, and I him. After hearing the inner workings of my brain, he called doctors at Harvard, Yale and Princeton. One day, he even brought in my ex-wife. She was painfully honest, though she was impressive.

Perhaps I truly am unique, but what does it say about you when you are your shrink's prize pupil? Good? Bad?

This morning once again I'm running at the river, the best shrink's couch on the planet, and I'm still asking myself those questions. How are your thoughts? Are you staying busy? Are you repairing any damage you may have caused? Are you laughing enough? Loving enough?

I'm still loving his voice and and the fact he prescribed very few pills. Instead he worked with words, comfort, and this thing called hope. Hope, you see, is a good thing. A really good thing.

I'm writing this to say thanks to a man who's no longer on this side of the ground; am wanting to thank someone I fear can't hear me. I'll sum up my gratitude and this essay the way our relationship closed. It went down like this:

It was his last day on the job. His office was cluttered with boxes and pictures torn off walls, papers scattered, a shredder ready for the next job. I knew I was getting a little better because I wanted to leave a good impression, something that hadn't crossed my skull the last 18 months.

I was standing just outside his door, looking in. "Good-bye Dr. Rosen," I said. "I promise you I'm not going to think those thoughts anymore."

He didn't hesitate. "Yes, you are Dunn. They're just not going to bother you nearly as much. Have a great life."

And with that, Dr. Alvin R. Rosen walked back into his office, gave me one last look, and closed the door.

RIP

My Spot
(Finding Spirituality Through Carpool)

I have my spot.

I have my spot because seven years ago I answered an All-Staff e-mail. A teacher left – he used to work carpool. He went on to "pursue other ventures." Was anyone interested?

I wasn't, but I did have two things: the time and the need for money. I interviewed with Associate Head Rick Betts. No passion sparked within me, but somehow I convinced him. Maybe he felt sorry for me; maybe he liked me, I don't know, but somehow I outbid two other candidates.

All these years later and I'm still standing out here. My thoughts are on the guy who stood in that spot when I went to high school. He was mean, surly, threatening. He was scary. I would walk past him in fear and that would set the tone for my day. I would escape the fear of him only to sit in front of my teacher and my assignment and the fear would escalate times 12. Oh, how I hated that guy. On Halloween, I egged his house. He found out and never liked me.

Forty years later, I still don't give a damn.

Now, I get to NOT be that guy. I get to be the guy who sees people first. Here comes Emily Jacobs. She's a senior and she is all-ways (one word and two) tired! But she's always smiling. I love that. Grace Brock is right behind her. She, too, is always tired and often not smiling. That could be a challenge though, right?

Speaking of challenge, here comes Georgia Symbas. She always sees her cell phone first, traffic be darned. One day I caught her, gave her a bear hug and probably saved her life. She gave me an embarrassed grin. Now I have assigned her sister, Alex, the "Georgia responsibility ", cross first, cell phone later. We laugh about it now, it's a bond. And so far, we're all still here.

Jeff Klopfenstein's dad rolls down his window, he always does; he always needs the sports update. Many other parents are already on their own phones and wouldn't see me if I had on my Buddy the Elf costume. Emily Hingson's mom points at me with a knowing grin. One lady almost runs over me. This spot doesn't always come easy. And besides, sometimes it's cold! Why this morning, in fact, with the wind chill it was 2 degrees. Two! As in 1, 2.

Still, I have it at 85 percent, and Coach Stephen Jayaraj would be so proud of me for knowing that percentage. That's how many of them say "Thank you" to me for helping them do something they could just as easily do without me. Eighty-five percent. That's also how many of them thank me after a class of subbing. I read the lesson plan – it takes me 22 seconds max. Then I sit. Or I pace. And they thank me.

One day at carpool, Sophie Smith brought me a chicken biscuit. She had one left and thought of me out here in the cold. Her smile was warmer than the biscuit. I took it, we both left happy. Give and take is a beautiful thing. Often, Gracie Stovall brings me coffee, not because I'm me but because she's Gracie Stovall. She and I have discussed pole vaulting out here and the non-joys of chemistry class. Whether it's a good subject or a bad subject, she still giggles.

This warms me. I see this before her day kicks in. It's cold now and windy, but still I smile. She waves and walks in with her friend Victoria. Victoria nods, still asleep.

One day, Bryn Foster and I solved the third lap of the 1,600-meter run. She's good but we'll make her better. The third lap is the key. Later that afternoon, despite 25-mile per hour winds, she did it. She PR'd by seven seconds, third lap no problem. The smile on her face at the finish line said it all. It was so goofy cute and beautiful it almost made me wish I were back in carpool line again.

There comes Senior Dean Jason Rutledge; he always has that sneaky look on his face like we're about to share a morning joke. We usually do. Miller Kauffmann is walking up without his twin sister. She's always 200 yards behind and how they get that split up from South Campus is beyond me. Yet, it always happens. And it's okay.

When I applied eight years ago I didn't have a clue. Carpool? A spiritual thing? My friends pity me, even parents sometimes give me that "feel sorry for me" smile. They often pat me on the shoulder. I hate it when people don't get it. Perhaps for their punishment I'll withhold sending them my Bears Weekly Roundup newsletter. Yeah, that outta do it.

On this day, they're coming in late and in a hurry. I can still see the sleep Permabonded on their faces: It's a bad hair day for more than half (53%?). Some utter a hello; all have their agendas and the stress of it all has already kicked in. They are off. Their brains are computing, calculating. They all have jobs to do. So do I.

Because you see, I have my spot.

What Kids Don't Do; What Coaches Don't Coach

Ironically, I never learned this lesson while attempting to be an athlete; have never read about it in a coaching manual; never once heard it covered in a lecture. I'm not sure I've even seen it on SportsCenter.

No, I learned this from working carpool of all things. You see, I've been standing out there for nine years, though it seems like 109 on cold days. Trying to be a friendly soul, I always ask the kids how they're doing when they crest the Lower School parking lot hill and get up to me.

Unfortunately, they often do NOT say fine, or getting there, hanging in, or great. Instead eight of 10 of them utter two words. "I'm tired." I can assure you, these eight out of 10 statistics are NOT an exaggeration. If you don't believe me, stand out there with me one day – though bring a coat if it's winter. It can get pretty nasty out there.

Now I'm far from a doctor, ran as fast as I could from any science or math classes when I was a pup. Still, you don't need eight extra years of schooling to know that a tired body is an attractor factor for a cold, flu, bronchitis, strep throat and other illnesses. It's what keeps our beloved nurse Carolyn so busy;

there's no room for me to even stick my head in the door and say hi; maybe steal a cough drop. (This may sound trivial, but I RE-ALLY like my cough drops).

And let's not forget: A tired body is more likely to get injured. Oh, had I known when I was disguised as a marathon runner that rest equals training, that a day off would have surpassed a forced run. To steal the words of Kierkegaard: Life can only be understood backwards; but it must be lived forwards.

Then there's the snowball effect, the mental thing. A tired body and mind doesn't take in the information correctly in class; you're more apt to make bad decisions or utter the inappropriate comment. Gasp, your words may be a bit off this time of year when you're asking someone to Prom. This, as we all know, is simply not acceptable.

Personally, I'm still learning how to be a good cross country and track coach. I've got a five-star mentor in Stephen Jayaraj. I'm almost as passionate as he is, though I'm not the one who leads the talks or sets the tempo, and that's fine. Still, in this case, I'm going to be arrogant when I utter the three most important words I'll ever deliver as a leader – three words every coach and athlete needs to hear and write down.

Get. More. Sleep.

I'll go now. Have been at a track meet all day, taking down times and splits in the wind and the cold and the rain at Marietta High School. Was up early loading poles onto the van, grabbing tarps, finding the shot and discus bag, hoping not to get lost while driving to and fro.

In short, I'm tired.

Neugie's Nevers

Never get frustrated after leading the horse to water. You've done your part, now detach and move on.

Never interfere when women are planning a wedding. Sticking your head in a Weed Eater would perhaps be a better option.

Never have your second drink a completely different color from your first one. Mixing the colors mixes your brain in a hangover kind of way.

Never give a speech more than two pages long. For the record, one page equals four minutes, so when you get to page two, prepare to shut up. Be brief, be brilliant, be gone!

Never say yes when they ask, "Do you want this last piece?" because they do. They always do.

Never sit at the traffic light when you're turning left and the light turns yellow. As Lewis Grizzard once wrote: Make your turn on yellow or prepare a new life for yourself at the corner of Peachtree and Piedmont." Oh, how I miss Lewis...

Never ask them out on the phone when you can ask them to their face. It's harder to say no in person. Just sayin'...

Never hit "send" when you're upset. Sleep on it.

Never stand at the edge of the reflection pool at Berry College and toss a coin in while in a three-piece suit. You will fall in and everyone will laugh. Except for you.

Never listen when people say: "He won't bite", "You can't miss it", "What could go wrong", or "Just kidding."

Never say never is never always the answer; sometimes never is the answer. Example: starting a night with Jägermeister is never a good idea. Trust me.

Never draw a charge from a 200-plus pound man while playing intramural hoops. He can have the layup; you can have your health. Good trade if you ask me…

Never forget to hug your upcoming graduate. And send them peace – we all need it.

And finally, never forget to be kind. Those words came from the two wisest people to ever grace this planet, the Dalai Lama and my mother.

The Fourth Fact

No wonder our kids are confused. Take yesterday, for instance: April 20th. It was the anniversary of Columbine, a day 13 were killed in one of our schools. It was also our Prom Night, a time our kids celebrated their school and love for each other. Our youth participated in a walk-out, later went to Prom, on the same day. Love them and love this, but the reasons are adding up to walk out, march, make our statements.

Yesterday was also the birthday of Hitler, an egomaniac who inspired millions, therefore millions more were killed. And if all this weren't enough, April 20th also happens to be pot-based: Stoners gather to smoke lots of weed. There it is: death, love, greed and weed, all in one day.

This is our world – a place getting better and worse all at the same time. If you're talking elections, you may think the Trump-Hillary thing was the worst ever but think again. With social media, we're now trained to love one and hate the other – and with opinionated passions.

On the flip side, this is the same earth I feel warmth and beauty every day from simply walking our halls. Sure, we had prom, but I feel and see it on an odd Tuesday; it follows me home after cross country or track practice; makes me smile when I'm at home flipping channels.

Kids hear the experts on TV, but what do the experts know? Heck, I won the March Madness pool one year basing it on who had the prettiest uniforms. Or maybe it was the meaner mascot? We were supposed to put in money to enter and – Bo Hensley if you're out there – you still owe me twenty bucks to this very day.

I'm almost 58, and there's only three things I know for sure. First, you cannot throw up only once. Second, when two drunks start wrestling, they always end up fighting. And third, naps are underrated.

Other than that, I know that I know nothing – I'm taking this April 20th thing as living proof. I was home last night with my girlfriend, hoping I was heard when praying for the safety of our kids. Not only their physical bodies, but what they're growing up into.

There's so much out there, they need something to know – something to trust. A rock if you will. Politicians lie. Experts are wrong. National championship leads are blown. It's smoke and mirrors, so where do they turn?

Tarot cards? Bugs bunny? Weed? Guns and anger? CNN?

I'll close with my vote – my unsolicited opinion. I hope they quickly learn it all works from inside-out, not the other way around. Look within. Develop yourself. Work on self-acceptance and advance that to self-love. Soon that's all you'll have to work with so that's all you will say, do and project. You'll see and feel the results even in your Facebook posts.

In a sentence: It's all about taking your developing inner light – that inner peace and piece of God that is within you - and expressing it outward.

And that is the fourth thing I know to be true.

Writing, Anyone?

In 1984, I worked for a man named Pride Evans – I was disguised as an assistant tennis pro at Horseshoe Bend in Atlanta. Being the only single man on staff and being a little bit wild and crazy, I think Pride both identified with me and was perhaps wary of me at the same time. Anyway, this is what happened:

There was an upcoming tennis gig in Hilton Head; each country club was urged to send someone. Pride, being a wise man, decided NOT to send me. Good choice, though there was a problem: All the married and responsible adults had family plans, dinners, recitals, obligations. That left me. To quote from Pride when presented with this problem, "Oh (bleep)."

He called me in on a Thursday. Interesting I can remember things like this but I can be in the shower and not remember if I've washed my hair, but there it is. "Dunn," he said, "I'm sending you down to Hilton Head. HOWEVER, I want a typewritten report on my desk Monday morning. Sharp!"

Now I was 24, probably around 11 in maturity years and wet behind the ears in EVERY facet of life. All I heard was "Hilton Head…weekend!" I immediately called my friend – who drove a Porsche (this will factor in later). "We're going to Hilton Head, all expenses paid. Pick me up Friday at Horseshoe."

Long story short: We got lost on the way down, made it in past midnight, only to find out the tennis event was cancelled – attendance was down. "However, you gentlemen are welcome to enjoy your stay on Hilton Head – on the house, and thanks for your visit!"

What followed was this: golf car races, a shrimp boil though I'm not sure if we had any shrimp, board games, two late nights, a little tennis, and too much fun. On Sunday, we loaded up said Porsche and headed home on I-16.

And we were pulled over. Our car – two ownerships ago – had been stolen. Police thought we were running an illegal ring. Eight cop cars surrounded us – one put a gun to my back. The other put a gun to my friend's. Sirens. Fear. Peeing in pants. And then I remembered, "Oh (bleep), I've got to write this up!" More fear. More pee. Gun still in back. Jesus wept.

The miscommunication was cleared up and back home we went. Once back, I found myself sitting at my typewriter, still wetting my pants. What to do? Tell the truth? Lie my proverbial backside off? Tell him I misheard his orders and write a poem? Go to refrigerator and begin drinking? Again?

I wrote the truth, the whole truth and nothing but the truth so help me God. Left nothing out. Didn't try to make me the hero because I wasn't and I'm not. In diary form, it was four pages long, typewritten, double-spaced. Term paper teachers would have been so proud.

Monday, I waited until he was on the court. I sneaked in, put the papers on his desk, hid in the clubhouse locker room. Waited. Paced. Peed some more. No gun in back but none needed.

Eventually, I walked back to the tennis shop. Pride, bless his heart, had made a copy of my report; passed it out to everyone. They were laughing and enjoying something I had written.

I was hooked.

Game. Set. Match.

Keep Praying...Please

It seems a Washington court and school board suspended a football coach for taking a knee and praying at the 50-yard line after a game. Three "judges" ruled him guilty, said he was acting as a public official instead of a private citizen, therefore the school was justified in punishing him. To take this further, this means if you're Catholic, you can't even cross yourself.

Now even though I'm a writer, I'm not an opinionated soul. If nothing moves me, I'll never even reach for a pen. This, however, is too much. We live in a country of random bombings, mass hatred, shootings, political chaos and we are not allowed our BEST defense – praying to the heavens for guidance, for advice and for the love we all need? Really?

To the coach's credit, even though he was let go, he still bows and prays. God love him. May he prosper and go in peace. In the end, the Big Judge will declare him innocent, as should we all. He should never have been judged to begin with.

Me, I'm a small-town Georgia boy; call me a redneck and I'll take is as a compliment. We prayed every day before school, put our hands over our hearts and said the Pledge of Allegiance. Yes, we did this at a public place – my school. Yes, I'm a better person because of it. I still pray every day before my adventures at Holy Innocents'. Call me crazy but I hear God talking back. I have my game plan if you will – and the only way I can get it is to shut my mind up and let Him in. Again, I'm a better man because of it.

While on this subject, I googled the National Anthem this morning, wanted to know how long it was. Granted it's a tough question, since so many over sing the last verse and make it 10 minutes long. I sang it myself – in private whereas not to disturb the neighbors and get arrested for noise pollution. It took me one minute and six seconds. Personally, I don't think it's too much to ask to stand for one minute, six seconds before a game. If you choose to kneel, you do have that right.

In closing, I wish I were in Washington, wish I were seated before the very gavel in that court. I would love to be there while those "wise" souls glared into my God-loving eyes and declared me guilty.

Yes, I am guilty, damn guilty. But I can assure you I'll keep praying about it. And I hope the kids at my beloved school will, too.

Dunn Neugebauer
A Grateful American

Life is Fleeting

I know life is fleeting because I almost got run over this morning at carpool. A Ford Explorer almost took half the Rankin family and myself out of this earthly equation. If you're into demented ironies, Mrs. Rankin is our nurse.

Anyway, my last living thought would've been: I can't believe I forgot to turn down the heater!

Okay, nothing Socrates would pull me over for in the Great Beyond and wish to chat with me about, but there it was. Still, it got me thinking: I haven't even gotten started yet!

I want to live to be the oldest human on Earth never to turn on an iron. I want to watch the Falcons win the Super Bowl; witness term limits on Congress, and to address my state champion cross country runners at a banquet. I want to find my Nintendo and capture the queen in Super Mario Brothers; and live in a world where Prefontaine does win an Olympic medal and the bionic man marries the bionic woman. (How could that NOT have happened!). Finally, I want to see peace throughout it all, and I don't give a damn who the President is.

I'm grateful for this incident, though, for the great reminder. To paraphrase Cheryl Strayed in "Tiny Beautiful Things": "We're all going to die, so pound the bell like it's dinner time!"

Finally, I'm grateful again my time wasn't this morning. After all, my shirt was all wrinkled and my pants all dirty. Mother would have been simply appalled…

Another Peace Plea –
I'm Not Going to Stop

I made a deal with God a year ago. Told him I'd continue to spread peace, joy and humor on Facebook and, in return, He wouldn't make me do jury duty. You can laugh, as I still do, but so far both of us have kept our ends of the bargain.

About this gun thing…or is it a people thing…or is it both? You know, unfortunately, hate will always find a way. If it's not a gun, it'll be a knife. Or their fists. Or a tire iron. Or maybe it will be Colonel Mustard in the library with a rope. And if the hate's not enough, let's add in politics – throw Trump and Hillary into the mix and let's really get pissed off. There's all this fear going on and people are spreading their anger to cover it all up. Sad, but there it is.

I'm a political idiot: 57 years old and don't even know if I'm a Republican or a Democrat. After reading from both, I'm still not sure why I capitalized the first letters of either party. I have to look up the Amendments to know what they are and what they mean.

Yes, I'm a naïve soul – a dreamer if there ever was one. It's "colorful" now – perhaps got me beaten up a time or two in high school. Still, I don't like to write problems without solutions so I'll offer one.

It starts with the individual. Look in the mirror and learn to love what you see there. If you don't, then you're being just plain rude. It is that simple. The Heavens gave you this gift...and you hate it? You want to be someone else? You matter. He made it so, and you're complaining? I'm telling you to start loving what you see, and then spread that love faster than a political opinion on Facebook. Jump on it like a fumble on a pro football Sunday afternoon. Yes, it starts with me – it starts with you.

Be the change, Gandhi said that, and I'll be damned if I'm ever going to argue with him.

I'll conclude – I feel your anger at long posts (See? Anger again!) Granted I'm writing this from the context of a posh private school. Classrooms here are bigger than my condo. I can move in and still have room for two end tables and a couch.

I'll be arrogant as I conclude – I'll start with me. The bell just rang. I'm about to walk out of the library, out a set of double doors and into another building. Up some stairs, down the hall, and into the third room on the left. I'll pass about 150-220 of our 528 Upper School students. Maybe walk past 10 adults or so.

Fear not. You don't have to worry about me. The only weapon I'll be carrying is my smile...

Peace, always peace!

Weekend at Bernie's – Part Dunn

I'm not apologizing for this – when you say thank you it needs to be said in as clear a way as possible. I was driven to this keyboard because I've never known how to appropriately thank someone who – and I'm getting somewhat dramatic – may have saved me.

I've had ten years to think about it and I still don't know how to thank this guy. It's one of the reasons I get mad when I see the media constantly portraying all these bad, mean, corrupt people, these pampered athletes, when there are SO many good people out there. I'm telling you, there are angels down here; they're dressed like you and me, they look so normal, you wouldn't be able to make them out in a crowd.

Like this guy.

He's probably dressed in running shorts, a T-shirt and a hat as I write this. He probably woke up this morning and, please read this, his day's agenda had little or nothing to do with himself. It was running here to help her; training this lady there; helping someone move into their new place here; picking up somebody else because her car was acting up.

This person has no self. It's all about you. And you. And what do you need? Can I help you?

Anyway, there was a six-month period in my life when I was Bernie from the 1989 movie classic *Weekend at Bernie's*. You probably remember the idea: Bernie was dead, so all his friends just picked him up and moved him around from place to place, activity to activity.

I felt dead. Not totally, but if you've ever been depressed you may remember that paralyzing feeling, where the thought of doing ANYTHING sounded horrible. Right off the bat, your mind gave you 27-plus reasons why you couldn't even load the dish washer.

Without carping on about what I've carped on too many times before, this friend took me in after my divorce. Briefly, here was my life picture: five figures in credit card debt; little to no work; no drive; no ambition; no real home. To sum it up, I was a medical flat line. If you know me now, you wouldn't have then. I wouldn't have noticed you; I wouldn't have made the effort; would've only grunted at you if you said hello to me.

All you beautiful people out there, you wonderful Facebook friends, so honest and loyal and passionate? I would've known not a one of you.

Anyway, my friend picked Bernie up by his shirt collar one day and pointed to his couch. When it was dinner time, he picked me up and put me at the dinner table. On lucky nights, I got a smoothie. If I was good (though I was neither good nor bad), I'd get the leftover part that was still in the blender.

One day, he loaded me up and we traveled across the state to look at manatees. One night it was off to some film festival. It was a John Maxwell seminar one weekend. One Saturday, we helped Carolyn move. A word here: I wouldn't know Carolyn if she walked up to me right now and bit me on the back side and I hate moving on a good day. But when you're depressed, you hate doing anything. So why not help Carolyn move? So, I did.

Most nights, my friend's job was to lock up an apartment complex in Juno Beach. He pointed to the hot tub and I got in while he made his rounds. When the time was up, he put me back in the car, took me home, gestured towards his couch.

He asked me for nothing. Not for rent. Not a favor. Not to borrow my car. Not to buy him dinner (had no money anyway). He didn't resent me or anything I stood for. I was a shell of half of a man and he helped. Because that's what angels on Earth do. That's who they are.

One day I came home proud. I'd gotten a part time job at Barnes & Noble (hated it!) and had a little money. I offered him $300 to help him with his rent. Three hundred dollars rent in West Palm will generally get you about five nights, but it was all I had. He simply smiled, accepted it, thanked me; then fixed me dinner.

Not that I have a good memory, but on May 6, 2007, I got the call to come home back to Holy Innocents'. I cried. No, I'm not macho, I cried. I was going home, to the greatest kids in the world, to the state where October has the best weather ever, to the erratic Braves, to traffic jams on I-285, to my favorite Dunkin Donuts in the city.

I packed quietly, left like a thief in the night on May 30, 2007 – my 47th birthday. I didn't want to wake him up, I didn't get to say thank you. I didn't get to tell him how much I appreciate him for who he is, what he did and what he all-ways does. I didn't get to tell him that he might've saved my life.

Anyway, when I feel clueless or confused, all I know to do is go to the written word. He's not on Facebook so he won't read this. And I won't mention his name, but his initials are Brian Bahe. And if any of my West Palm buds down there, if you even remember who I am, I'd love it if you'd hand him this story. I've been trying to reach him for the last two years but his mailbox is full and I don't have his email address.

As I said, there are angels among us. They look just like you and me. Thankfully, Bernie has woken up and he walks the halls at Holy Innocents', not a proud man but a grateful one. My arrogant statement is simply that I'm one of the the luckiest among us.

91

Also, as I said, 10 years have passed and I still don't know how to say thanks. After all, how do you thank someone who asks for nothing while he offers up his home, his food and his care, no questions asked, until you get your life back? Is there a monetary value on your life?

I'll close like this, for better and for worse. They say your memory fades as you get older. Mine hasn't. Women and elephants have nothing on me. As I write stories about my beloveds, sub in the classroom, carry on in carpool and coach my sports, I don't forget. I'll never forget.

Thanks for being even better than the smoothies you make, and that's the nicest thing I can ever say about anybody. Thanks for being the most selfless person I've ever met. Though I hope you won't ever need me to return the favor, I hope your life stays great, I will do my best to pay it forward.

You taught me that. You made me a better person. You saved me.

From as deep in my heart as I can go, thanks! All-ways, thanks!

Dunn Neugebauer, a.k.a. Bernie

The Little Things

I'm standing on the track infield, just watching. I do this often, it's the writer in me. My girls are in one stretching circle, my boys about eight yards away in another. It's Friday, they are laughing, happy – a bunch of active verbs pausing before their weekend.

It seems Bryn and Lexi are going hiking. Berkley's still on this spirit animal thing. Liam can't run a cool down without putting on a pair of swim fins. James is running, literally, between track and soccer.

This running thing has made them close; earned them friends. If you want to get competitive, their times are dropping, improvement showing in every pair of feet.

Perhaps my point is gratitude. If you edit yourself in your job interview, you're applying for the wrong job. Same in relationships. There is no editing out here. It's all fresh, random, out from left field. Adults often tell you a joke just to set you up before selling you something. It's better here. These kids are only being who they are. They haven't learned to act on behalf of a company and I'll be damned if I'm going to teach them that.

Education is often defined as the art of drawing out from, NOT putting into. Walking our halls is like being in an Improv comedy class. They tell you something; you must respond and keep the conversation going. If it stops, you failed.

The beauty is in being random, as they are. Speak your truth. Enjoy your rhythm. Find your own voice. Earlier, for example, I was in the halls and I caught Gracie playing in the water fountain. Cute. Adorable. Spencer gave me a high-five though I'd done nothing to deserve it. Several walked past, no eye contact, brains working so fast I could literally see the wheels spinning. It's all a good rhythm, a chaotic, random as heaven rhythm.

It's gratitude for the little things, and not necessarily believing what people often try to sell you. I've learned not to just accept things simply because I've always heard it, and not to accept it when people say millions of people can't be wrong. Sure, they can. Ten million people bought the album *Saturday Night Fever*. Seventy-five thousand paid to see WrestleMania in the Pontiac Silverdome. Nixon was elected in a landslide.

It's about copying the good, discarding the bad, adding seeds of your own. Listen to Jackson Browne's song, *For a Dancer*. He describes this very well. I must close now. After all, my "verbs" are drifting away from the track and headed into tonight, which will assuredly blend into their adventures of tomorrow. Lots of walls I'd like to be flies on, but it doesn't work that way.

I'm grateful they are here and I must be just as grateful to, one day, let them go. That's hard – man that's hard. Maybe I do know a little of what it's like to be a parent. Still, I smile. They are getting better. They are bonding. If they never change, it's okay with me. I hear them laughing.

I turn back for one last look... and they are gone.

The Little Things – Part II

It ain't the big things in life it's the little things. And sometimes these little things don't even need to be said. My days aren't marked by merits but by memories. Here are some worth sharing...

One day at carpool, one of my runners, Erin Hill, brought me a doughnut. She even inscribed the box "To Coach Dunn." It was so cute I almost didn't throw the box away after I'd eaten. The simple gesture lightened my step; elevated my spirits.

Years ago, Jordan McBride was headed to class. I'm in the hall, about to go to mine. She was tired, suffering from the winter blues. Not a word was spoken, though she walked up and tucked her head into my shoulders, an armless hug if you will. I patted her head, gave her a smile. She walked into class. This was an incident so simple, I almost didn't put it in here. But why have six years gone by and I haven't forgotten it? And I won't.

One season, I came upon a painfully shy runner named Graham on mile four. For those not into running, the endorphins can be like having a couple of drinks, and this shy kid started talking. Anyway, Graham would NOT stop talking on this day. He spoke of the joys of scuba diving, how he loved being down there; the peace; the wonderfully alone feeling. I would pass him in the hall from that day forth, and I won't lie, he didn't become outgoing and we didn't become buds. Still, one day he wanted to share his love for his hobby with someone. It was me. And now, after all the miles I've run, that one remains one of my favorites.

Two years ago, a girl wandered into a classroom at lunch. A teacher was in there, listening to music. They both randomly started singing. Kids in the hall heard the music, joined in. An idea was born. Every Friday, to this very day, you can go into Room 406 in Groesbeck Hall and have a jam session. There are drums, guitars, harmonicas, sometimes even animals in there. But there is always noise, beautiful noise, and I can't help but notice they're all walking a little easier as they head to their last class.

And finally, there is my dad, and the day my pitiful self was leaving Madison heading back to Atlanta. About how, completely out of context, he walked me to my car, put his hand on my arm and said, "I'm with you, you hear?" And how that one simple gesture changed everything between us, everything for the better.

Erin brought her coach a doughnut. Jordan needed a hug. Graham just wanted to talk to somebody. A girl sang because it seemed the natural thing to do. And one day, in Madison, Ga., a father gave his son a reassuring pat on the shoulder.

Little things?

I think not.

Have a great weekend...

Believe!

We've all heard people say, "You've got to believe." The bottom line is, you really do.

I've come to know that THE difference, in most if not all cases, between people who succeed as opposed to people who don't is belief. Period. The ones that make it, quite simply, know they can so they keep on until they do.

They're not more talented; not smarter; not more blessed. They are just stubborn, in the good way.

You've heard the stories: Walt Disney went bankrupt seven times before he became, well, Walt Disney. Wayne Dyer bought every printing of his first book, put them in his trunk, and drove across the country getting on small radio stations in promoting it. Why small stations? The large stations wouldn't have him on because nobody knew who he was.

J.K. Rowling scribbled Harry Potter tales on the backs of napkins while working in a coffee shop. I'm even taking this analogy to animals: Bumblebees' wings are technically so small they shouldn't be able to fly, at least very well. Nobody bothered to tell them, though, so...off they go.

My favorite of these stories, however, is the one about Sylvester Stallone. He was dirt poor, wrote the script for *Rocky* over a weekend. Producers loved it, made him lucrative offers for it. He wouldn't budge. After all, the deal was HE had to play the starring role.

"You're too short."

"You talk funny."

"You're not a boxer."

He held on to his belief, in his script and in himself. You know the rest of this story. Someone else also believed in him and thus, Sylvester Stallone became...Rocky – in what is arguably the best sports movie ever.

A valid question: How do you believe if you don't believe? My thoughts: We are all an idea from the heavens – sent down on a mission that we can accomplish. Key word – can – He didn't put us down here to fail. Also, hiding your light under a bushel and living small does no good.

The fact that you exist is the definition of the word belief all by itself. If you saw your reflection in the mirror this morning, there is your proof. And if you want to know what's the point of all this - you are. You are the point.

In closing, I witnessed some belief Saturday on the track. One of my girls, we'll call her Jackie since that's her name – doesn't have the science of running down, yet. Still, if a Learjet took off from the starting line, she would tear off after it. Why? Because she knows she can catch it. And I'll be damned if I'm going to tell her any different.

So, read all the books, hear all the speeches, gather all the information. When you go into your day, however, if you're not carrying that inner fire, you're not completing the mission God sent you down here to do.

Believe it.

Mental Health in 432 Words

I heard this is Mental Health Awareness week. Or if it's not, perhaps it should be. Maybe every week should.

I can speak for a small part of this. Don't judge me. We're all wacked somehow. Weird things set us off. I talk to myself. Mom used to assure me everything was okay when it wasn't. My girlfriend can't swim in a straight line. (Okay, that has nothing to do with mental health; I just find it cute). Here we are, warts and all. If we were perfect we'd have never been born.

Anyway, some people can't cross the t's or dot the i's. Some must be medicated. Some simply fixate, can't let go. What they're thinking about, in their own minds, is way more important than having conversations about the weather. Solution: They simply shut it out.

I can identify with the last bunch. If you need references, ask plenty of people who have been around me. I don't mind if they fill in the blanks, as long as they all know I mean well. Like I said, don't' judge.

Ironically, the first thing that popped into my head when I read about mental awareness was this snapshot of my life: I'm in Florida working the *Tampa Tribune* cryptogram. Usually, I never solved it, too much chaos. On this day, however, I did. The solution read: Everyone needs three things: Something to do, some-one to love, and something to look forward to.

This is key. No, this is major. My worst days were when I had little to do, knew I was in trouble when I was rearranging my sock drawer and looking forward to doing laundry. Second, if you can't find someone to love, then find *something* to love. Third, once these are solved, you all-ways (one word and two) have something to look forward to.

Perhaps the worst is that feeling that you're alone; glove and ball in hand but nobody to throw to. You are an idea in the mind of God, but, equally as important, so is everyone else. The trick is often to let go, particularly of the ones you love. Say yes. Under-stand your plan isn't the best one; we have such limited perspec-tive.

Finally, if you are breathing, you are needed. I must go now. I'm being summoned. One of our juniors, a random event wait-ing to happen, needs help with her essay. This is great. After all, I'm about to exercise my mental health in the best way humanly possible.

By helping somebody else.

More About this Mental Health Thing

Mental health month is ending. I say make June mental health month as well, maybe carry it forward into July, have a refresher course or two in the fall.

Mental Health: It's so in-the-news, so crucial, yet still so underrated. Whether these shootings are a gun problem or not, there's definitely a problem with the person holding the deadly weapon. I have no doctorate, I graduated without honors from Berry College, an undistinguished member of the Class of 1982. Moving forward, I couldn't even get into grad school, shocking with my 2.6 GPA.

Like it or not, I post my blog on Facebook. Sure, I have my ego, I often check to see if anyone reads it; anyone likes it. I've learned what works, what doesn't. And this is my astounding discovery: In November, 2016, I posted "Ode to a Depression," which chronicled my 18-month battle. The response was overwhelming: 10 and 20-fold what I was expecting or what I normally get.

And this is what I learned: Mental health needs to be written and spoken about. People thanked me for being transparent. Transparent? I was just doing my job as a human! People need to hear this: We are all, at one time or another, on common ground! Besides, who the hell wants to read or hear about someone who's perfect? Can anyone relate? Anyone?

God Bless any of you out there who have trouble even getting out of bed. Personally, as I've written, I once slept for a year-and-a-half and woke up in Pennsylvania. Don't judge yourself; you matter. God doesn't make mistakes.

Trust that you need the rest. You sleep better anyway, when you take a break without judgment. I look at it the Buddhist way: Don't just do something, lie there!

Sorry for the sermon, though I want to do my part. Reach out if needed. Run if needed. Take a walk when needed. Sleep when needed. You're not worthless; you're human. In fact, I'm off to take a nap right now. The difference between now and 11 years ago is I'm now perfectly at peace with it.

And I'm wishing you all that same peace…because you deserve it.

Happy Memorial Day and God Bless our veterans!

What Did You Learn?

My mother used to ask me that every day when I came home from school. Fifty years later, I've decided to answer her:

- I learned that it's hard to get back on the horse when you're still in midair from falling.
- I learned that a man's main job is to make sure his woman doesn't need another man. Period.
- I learned that, in the song *The Devil Went Down to Georgia*, the devil's fiddle is better than Johnny's. Sorry, just my opinion.
- I learned three great rules regarding public speaking: Be brief, be brilliant, be gone!
- I learned that if you can use common sense, you don't have to think. And that goes for more than just coaching.
- I learned that if you don't play your cards, God will shuffle your deck. I made that up all by myself and I'm sort of proud of it.
- I learned that the first time you talk to your ex-wife over the phone after your breakup is the most awkward call ever. There's always a pause at the end where you both used to say, "I love you."
- I learned to love alone time and to feel sorry for people who don't.

- I learned that, when you're trying to get into meditating, forget the books that tell you to start with 20 minutes. Start with one minute then work your way up.
- I've learned – when it comes to money – to be generous when you can, save when you can, and if you owe it, pay it.
- I learned that in coaching as well as in life, knowing when to shut up is often more important than knowing what to say.
- I learned that whoever invented Raid, the roach killer, knew what they were doing.
- I learned that if I'm going to sit down and have a few drinks, I'm not going to interrupt a perfectly good buzz by going to a movie. Pick one – not both.
- I learned to write it down. You'll look back on all this and wish you had.
- I learned that if people say they have a stomach bug, NEVER ask for details.
- I learned that when approaching a pretty woman or a new project, approach with confidence or don't approach at all.
- I learned I can tell a person's character by the way they treat a waiter.
- I learned that Columbo was the greatest detective ever.
- I learned how to get over my ex-wife, but never how to get over my dog.
- I learned that most people that sing the National Anthem over sing it.
- I learned I always get mad at people with hidden agendas, relief pitchers that can't throw strikes and people that don't turn left at yellow lights.

- I learned that everyone is normal until you get to know them.
- I learned to keep it simple – almost if not always.
- I learned when you're in a relationship, and the girl tells you to "sit down, we need to talk;" that when you stand back up, you're probably no longer in a relationship.
- I learned that if you love your job and someone asks how many hours you put in a week, you have no idea how to respond. If you hate your job, you could answer down to the minute.
- I learned that if I go to a postseason Atlanta Braves game, they will always lose.
- I learned that if you go to a toga party, always put something on underneath. I know this from experience – fortunately not my own.
- I learned to be careful of the punch at a college party. There's no telling what a bunch of fraternity brothers will put in there.
- I learned to call her, even if she's out of my league. If nothing ese, I can always brag that I tried.
- I learned never to play cornerback in flag football wearing Docksides. I know this from experience and yes, it was my own.
- I learned that if you can't figure out which twin to ask out, ask the least popular one. She's usually the most down-to-earth.
- I learned never try to play intramural basketball when you have a hernia. Fouling out will be the least of your problems.
- I learned never to throw up in my roommate's car. It tends to put a damper on the relationship.
- I learned to get to the point.

- I learned that the milk and the cereal rarely run out at the same time.
- I learned that a good pair of loafers will last at least four years.
- I learned to set my limit when it comes to my waist size.
- I learned that figuring out how and where to get rid of a couch is more complicated than buying one and having it delivered.
- I learned that the more people there are on a committee or in a meeting, the worse the final decision.
- I learned that sports brings out the best, and the worst in people.
- I learned that high school can be tough. It's not like the movie *Grease*, where you meet a hot blonde on the first day and then dance on top of cars the whole time.
- I learned that as a kid, getting a physical was the most routine thing ever. As you get older, not so much.
- I was supposed to learn that a journalist shouldn't get too close to the story he's working on. I don't agree. I learned you should jump all in the middle of it. How else can you truly write about it?
- I learned that if I'm doing the word jumble in the daily paper and the words look fine the way they are, then I probably had too much to drink the night before.
- I learned that since the world is round, then there's no way there can be any such thing as north, south, east or west. My geography teachers never understood this philosophy. Just sayin'.

- I learned to have a general plan but rarely a specific one.
- I learned that making a pretty woman laugh is one of the best feelings there is.
- I learned that when two drunks start wrestling, they always end up fighting.
- I learned that often the best thing to do is simply sit back and let karma do its thing.
- I learned that a drunk comment is a sober thought.
- I learned that when people say, "We should get together sometime," you probably never will.
- I learned that I love to stay in hotels. And I don't care if that's weird or not.
- I learned that loving yourself is way more important than you may think.
- I learned that the worst part about a biopsy is the dreading it beforehand.
- I learned two things in life will humble you; marriage and marathons.
- I learned there is no such thing as "getting a good seat" when you're going to a meeting.
- I learned to travel only with people I like a lot or love, no exceptions.
- I learned when enough is enough, so I'll move on now.

Happy Father's Day

I just ran at the river and thought of you, Dad. I actually heard you tell me to go faster but I can't. Still, I'm picturing you in your room listening to Beethoven, drawing some beautiful scenery. Nothing personal, but I'm sure your room is an absolute pigsty. Why should anything change?

Anyway, these are the things I want to tell you:

We had 37 years together; lived in the same house for 18. Mom used to try and wake us up for school. Love her to death but her soft, Southern voice proved to be the Worst. Alarm Clock. Ever. But then, you stepped in.

You would reach in the dirty clothes and pull out the socks you'd worn the day before. You would then throw them on my nose. Worst. Smell Ever. Remember the cartoon scene, the one where the person is asleep and suddenly they're fully awake and on their feet? That was me.

Another one: One day I had to get back to Atlanta. Had things to do, lessons to teach, women to get rejected by. I had my keys in hand and suddenly, you asked if I wanted to go play a round of golf. Not coming up with a reason not to, I said yes...so off we went.

At the pro shop, the manager tried to give you a scorecard and you wouldn't take it. "We don't need one," you said. Great move on your part.

Because we simply played. Drove off the tee. Looked for my ball. Hit it again. Looked for my ball. Eventually putted in; proceeded to next hole. Father. Son. Golf.

You know, some things are just pure. Nothing else to be said.

Which brings me to my last one. In my Little League days, I had many adventures. I pitched the only game my team lost one year. Witnessed Bill Ashburn's 7-base single (and I'm not kidding). The only homer I hit there were at least three errors committed; the final one being the umpire ruling me safe at the plate.

One day you came home from work tired and you saw me playing with my glove; throwing the ball in it and pounding away. You asked me to go outside and play catch.

Now, I try not to be touchy-feely, but remember the final scene in *Field of Dreams*? When Kevin Costner plays catch with his dad? Again, pure stuff. It's almost like the Heavens sometimes call a time out, from life, from everything, to make you slow down and enjoy the little things.

I often write of little things; try to appreciate them every day. Still, 37 years. I played golf with you once, just you and me. We played catch in the yard. These are things that stand out. And I'm looking forward to doing it again, except for the part about the socks. How about a tee time in 2050?

Again, no scorecard required…

Love always,

Your #3 son

Forgiveness and a Scene at the Door

I remember when I thought it was over, or I wished it was.

Get the picture: Double date, 1975. I'm walking her to the door. I'm nervous; hear music playing in the background. I feel like Kevin on the *Wonder Years*. The big moment. How to handle this? Aggressive? Passive? A hug and then move in quickly?

Inspired by a recent 44-point performance by "Pistol" Pete Maravich and the disappearance of a giant zit that once rested atop my forehead, I went for it. And…she turned her head and I kissed her in the left ear. The other couple I was double-dating with saw the whole thing. In short, it was public knowledge by lunch the next day.

If there were social media, this would've been on Facebook, Instagram and Snapchat, with texts flying everywhere. Oh, the pains of being 15, walking back to the car while the other two were in the back seat were laughing their collective butts off. The walk of shame. Ah, I know it so well.

Fast forward to present: I was given some good advice yesterday by our Head Chaplain here at school. I had a recent misadventure that caused a little pain; ruined my sleep and a couple of my nights at my watering hole. This is not acceptable.

He stopped me before I could tell him what happened. He's

heard it before and he'll hear it again; didn't need to hear it this time.

"I helped you last year and you're still here," he said. "The FIRST thing you need to learn is to don't let this stop you from being you. In the end, if you're wronged somehow, it's on them."

I'm rattling this around in my skull, coming up with a life lesson. Okay, the girl didn't wrong me. She was protecting her reputation in high school land. And, I was such a boy; such a tool. The couple that told the couple that told him that told her, they were just being their 15-year-old selves. No animosity there. I would've done the same thing; in fact probably did. Fair is fair.

Recently, though, not so much, someone was at fault. There is evil out there. Forgiveness, so easily written and talked about, not so easy when it's your turn to be the one forgiving. Eventually, I return to keeping it simple so it comes down to this:

I've got a date with my girlfriend Saturday night. I'm walking her to the door. I still get a bit nervous about these things. The moon and stars will glance down to give me a 1-through-10 rating. Birds will wake up to possibly get a good laugh. God will hide his eyes, I've put Him through this before. Regardless, even if she looks left at that pivotal moment, I will keep going; I won't look back.

After all, as the saying goes, I ain't going that way.

Life in 527 Words or Less

In my opinion, the stupidest comment ever: Came from a parent while I was packing for college. "I certainly don't envy you!" That was so wrong I still recall it to this day, and wish I could forget it.

Scariest memory: Being on stage, disguised as a comedian down in West Palm, telling my BEST joke and not hearing a sound. Not one laugh. No snicker. Not even a golf chuckle. It's the same as saying the "L" word to your date and waiting to hear it back. And waiting…and waiting…and waiting…

Something cool: My unofficial niece made an imprint of her hand in the middle of her journal. Why, I asked? "That's easy," she said. "Whenever I'm having a bad day, I open up to that page and give myself a high five. It makes me feel better."

Something to tell your kids: When you hit your golf ball in the woods and then find it with a snake coiled up around it: Don't pick it up. Trust me, there are worse things in the world than two-stroke penalties…

Something to remember: "If it resonates within you, write it down!"

Something to forget: That Super Bowl, when the Falcons blew that huge lead.

Four beings I'd have liked to spend some or more time with: Jesus, Robin Williams, Red Forman of *That 70s Show*, and my old dog Jasper.

Four things I'd like to never argue about again: Donald Trump; Georgia vs. Georgia Tech; men vs. women; and Batman vs. Superman

Heaven is: A run on a 60-degree day; a day with a good book; a night by a fire; and climbing under a blanket on my couch with my computer next to me.

Hell is: Listening to congressmen; manipulative people; lumpy beds; cold soup; running out of red wine, and having to say goodbye after a great time or trip.

Best song lyrics: "Let the disappointments pass, let the laughter fill your glass, let your illusions last until they shatter. Whatever you might hope to find, among the thoughts that crowd your mind, there won't be many that ever really matter." – Jackson Browne

Quote to live by: "Be kind whenever possible; it is always possible." – Dalai Lama

Biggest mistake(s) I ever made: Hurrying through high school and college. I remember standing with both diplomas in my hand and asking, "Now what?" (FYI – I still ask that!)

Something important I've learned: When the guy at the Mexican restaurant puts your plate down in front of you and tells you the plate is hot, believe him…

Another something: When somebody rips into you and then tells you they're just kidding, don't believe them. They're not.

And finally, something I know: If time flies when you're doing it and you forget to eat because you're loving it, then THERE is your passion and THAT is what you should do for a living.

A Cute Slice of Life

The last day our girls' cross country team goes to the river before 'race day', they veer off the beaten path into the opposite direction. Instead of the three-mile trail formerly rated as one of the nation's best, they head backwards.

Moving through the parking lot, they go up the ramp we'd just driven down and take a left over the bridge. Here, the scenery gets interesting: If you look right, you see the hustle of the big city, an access road with I-285 behind it, bumper to bumper cars, the sound of horns, brakes, even car radios.

Looking left, however, you see the calm of the Chattahoochee; rafts floating; ducks on cruise control. Often, I laugh at this point, as my mood can change simply by which direction I gaze. Thankfully, most days I choose the river, and I'd like to think my days pass easier because of it.

The girls cross the bridge and go left into another parking lot. There are bathrooms here, picnic tables, extra parking spaces for those that couldn't fit on the "main drag." If you keep going far enough, more trails lead into the woods.

I'm not familiar with the tree the girls choose, but they have one. And off that tree each girl picks a leaf.

"You hold on to your leaf and when you run back across the bridge, you have to stop, make a wish and then throw your leaf into the river," one of my runners, Bryn Foster, later told me. "If you see it all the way down into the water, your wish will come true. If you don't, it won't."

I have no idea how these girls came up with this, though I have a long-held respectful opinion of the spontaneity and the creativeness of the teenage mind. Many adults make the mistake of "trying to figure it out." Don't do this, I say. Simply observe and enjoy. Write it down if you want; it can be used as entertainment; stories to tell at parties.

After all, they are busy, fresher from God. Day in and day out it's a hustle. I laugh while picturing this: Eight runners leaning over the bridge, some practically falling over. Each following her leaf as it swings with the wind, twisting, turning. Each set of eyes following their own, hoping their wish comes true whether it be a Prom date, an A grade, a better relationship, or a new car on their upcoming birthday.

I can sense their anticipation, can feel their hopes, their youth. I'm often envious of their adventures and their courage and their confidence as they pound their way into something new without forethought.

On this day, these eight trot back onto the "normal" side of the river, their workout done for the day. I hear them before I see them – Megan Roddenbery is telling a story about the perils of senior portraits and all it stands for. The other seven are straight across in listening, even though they've often been told to go two-by-two. They hear and they understand, but a good story is a good story; all are looking at their co-captain while she explains how she screwed up a perfectly good picture and boy, won't mom be appalled.

They circle around me as they get back, and, out of habit already starting to stretch. I don't ask about their leaves; I don't because I understand their resilience. Whether their leaf got hurled under the bridge or whether they saw it down, they are already off to other things, more adventures.

The leaf-dropping was SO five minutes ago, a lifetime in teen-age world. Instead I remain mute, watch them stretch, listen to them giggle.

After all, there will be other runs on other days. Soon eight more leaves will twist through the air. Eight girls will bend over and stare down, their dreams oh-so-temporarily depending on the result as they wish, hope.

My job is simply to smile and live for this...and keep watching my own leaf as it arcs downward toward the river.

Welcome to My Weirdness

Someone once wrote that we're all cracked, but that's how the light gets in. I have a friend who keeps saying that everybody is normal until you get to know them. With this said…

My granddad was a Baptist preacher, so I grew up with Jesus, the Bible and Christianity. An avid reader, I devoured the New Testament, though the Old was a bit much for me. Instead I re-read the New. Two things stood out:

First, giving thanks in advance. And second, and this is the big one, when Jesus said, "All these and even greater things can you do."

We'll get back to that. To give you some context, I believe firmly that we humans are "two-thirds" people. First, we hear or read something; that's easy. Second, we understand it; that's usually simple as well. It's the third part, the putting it into play, where we have a problem.

With all that said, this is what happened: I was having a bad day at school, struggling with a relationship and not happy with the negativity I was feeling. Part of my weirdness is in ending things with people on a good note; you never know if you'll see them again.

Anyway, I'm subbing in the library – lamenting, pouting, overthinking. At the desk, I spotted a stack of 4-by-6 yellow note cards and the brain kicked into overdrive. Who are we? Why do we read this stuff and not act on it? Are these just words? Was this Jesus guy serious?

I picked up the top note card and I wrote this: *Dear Heavens, thank you SO much for resolving this issue, for the betterment of all involved. I feel so much better and I really appreciate who and what you are and all the love you bring. Sincerely, Dunn.*

With that, I folded the note and put it in my back pocket. And within an hour, everything was resolved. Had a great conversation with the person in question. Walked away happy, peaceful, smiling.

Coincidence? The critic within made me try it again…and again. And it kept working. My last note was written May 9th of 2018. *Thank you for finding a buyer for our house; I am grateful that everything worked all for all involved. You rock.*

Within nine days, the house was under contract.

Has this worked every time? No. But guess what? Every time it didn't work, something better came along right behind it. I remember telling this "note card" story to a friend. He politely smiled, probably thought me crazy, said nothing.

However, within weeks he would often call and ask if I'd "note card" something for him. Eventually, I think, he has become a believer.

My conclusion: Why read positive, spiritual stuff simply as something in a book? Why not believe it, trust it, act on it? Personally, even if I weren't a believer, I must believe my very own experience, right? It works. The written word has power. Gratitude has power. Belief has power.

All these and even greater thing, just words? Are our thoughts and words way stronger than we think? Are we more powerful than we think? Will we die and learn that our solutions were simply at the tip of our tongue; and/or at the stroke of a pen?

I honor your beliefs. As for me, I will give thanks in advance to the God I believe in.

And to honor my own, I will write on yellow note cards and stick them in my back pocket.

A-men...

Grateful, and Here's Why

It's been more than 11 years since I've gotten back. Eleven years.

I can still remember filling out the paper work in front of Rick Betts' desk, dotting all my I's and crossing all my T's, not wanting to get left out. It was my birthday, May 30, and I purposefully planned my drive up from Florida so I would always remember the day I came back home to Atlanta.

Our baseball team was in the process of winning its first state championship at that time, but I had no connection; knew none of the kids. I felt lost, like a rudderless ship or a people person with no one to talk to. In short, I was a pretty sad case.

Still, I was excited, very much so, though I had ZERO clues what the years ahead would hold. I had no idea that the very ringing of a bell would excite me like Pavlov's dogs, releasing me into the hallways among the energy of the high school kids. I never knew that the morning of the first day of cross country practice would have me up before the alarm – summer vacation be damned. I never knew the simple act of opening my computer at home and writing up the football game that just happened could be so much fun. And just the thought of it still gives me that warm and fuzzy feeling.

Let's get something straight up front: – As a writer I've never had much a problem taking journalistic liberties. Call me a yellow journalist if you want to. Still, I don't know if I'm going too far overboard when I say that my job, these kids, this coaching, this writing, has saved and still is saving my life. NEVER have I jumped out of bed at 5 in the morning for anything. Now I'm up and ready to go and my only regret is that Dunkin Donuts doesn't open earlier.

It's March as I write this. We're back from Spring Break only to be faced with another week of winter. The kids are all suntanned, peeling even, from their beaches and pools and excursions. Stories fill the hallways while the lockers are again slamming and the flirting revs back to full throttle.

I watch all of this with a smile on my face. No, it's not the real world, but who cares? Our real world and our country has turned into a Dave Barry novel, except all the anger isn't close to being funny. I wish George Carlin were still alive; his comedic genius and his spin on this would be welcome to EVERYONE, Trump or no Trump. I miss Robin Williams, too, as well as the written words of Pat Conroy, and of course, the encouragement from both my parents even when I was a lost soul.

Dad's the one who gets lots of credit for moving me forward, you know? I was jobless years ago, failing at every facet of life, going nowhere and no money even to cry in my beer I couldn't afford. When walking to my car in my hometown of Madison to go back to Atlanta, Dad usually waved from the living room, said his goodbyes while going back to his artwork.

This day was different. He walked me out, I found this odd. After listening to Mom be Mom and reminding me to comb my hair, brush my teeth, look nice, call often, etc., Dad simply walked forward, extended his hand, put it on my shoulder.

"I'm with you, you hear?" That was all he did; that was all he said. I will tell you now, years later, that when his hand touched my shoulder my entire relationship with my father – not to mention my life – changed. Electricity went up my arm. He then became one of my best friends, and I went onward with a confidence I'd never had, and I often still lose.

Such a simple act it is, an extended hand placed on one's shoulder. Who knew?

On this rainy day, I have no anger to share with any of you, only thanks. In the overall scheme of things, we don't have many problems. Why, the fact that we showered this morning puts us ahead of 85% of the people on this planet. That makes us rich, people, that makes us rich.

I am rich and I am grateful. I have a school to go to. Bells are ringing; adrenaline fills this place. Boy is meeting girl and completely screwing it all up, but he'll dust himself off and try again three times before this month's up. Someone is bombing a quiz and will soon tear it up in anger; but will be texting again in eager anticipation before lunch. Coaches are meeting with players and trying to make sense of the season past or the one going on. Eager anticipation, for one thing or another, is the order of the day. It is every day. I live for this energy, this mindset.

Yes, I couldn't agree with Pat Conroy more when he wrote about teaching school. "No one ever warned me that I'd fall in love with all of my students; and every graduation would be like the death of a small civilization."

In summary, I'm grateful for the life of it all, the noise, the balls bouncing, chalk scribbling on the boards, kids taking five-star, drool-infested naps while trying to stay awake. It's adorable, all of it is, and I'm nostalgic about it even though I'm still here. That makes no sense, but there it is.

I'll go now, but Dad, let me share this with you before I'm off. I still screw up more than my share, but I can all-ways, one word and two, feel your hand touching my shoulder. It's there now, but I must temporarily remove it. I must go.

After all, the bell just rang…

Nineteen Minutes, Fifty-Two Seconds

0:00 - She seems so calm, which I find a bit odd. Usually on race day, or Vision Quest day as I have often referred to it, you are antsy times 12 mentally and physically.

We're on I-20 if that matters. It's early; cross country early as we like to say. It's the dynamic of the sport. Football players go off to torture in the summer for camp. Baseball players spend spring break somewhere in Florida. Basketball troops spend Thanksgiving and Christmas holidays traveling to tournaments. Well? Cross country runners get up at dark-thirty on Saturday mornings and run in exotic fields across the state.

It's what we do.

Now let me back up even further. She is sophomore Bryn Foster. Her quest is to break the 20-minute barrier in the 5K. She's been close, close enough to continue to pour gas on the fire of her dream. And she's been frustrated because she hasn't made it yet.

We've talked about these near misses. "You're almost there!" "Don't quit!" I even tried my hand at being a Star Wars, Yoda-like character when I told her: "Trust the journey!" These are some of my texts, but like emails, they usually get deleted in my normal clear your clutter, clear your mind manner.

I check my mirror to look at all my kids. Pre-race or pre-game rituals have always fascinated me. I love to see how they get motivated. Some rock out, pace, punch things. Others sit silently, gazing off into forever. Some joke and gather around. Others go into solitude.

I want mine to be pumped, edgy, anxious.

For now, though, most of them are asleep. Jesus wept.

I laugh to myself as I change lanes, about these kids, this sport, this generation. It's these differences and habits of the teenage mind that keeps me loving what I do. The kids of today aren't bad, they're just a bunch of hyperactive verbs. Verbs do things, they say things, they're busy. You want a conversation with a kid in the hall? Don't expect them to stop, they've got places to go. You either speak quickly or you walk with them.

The old-fashioned sort might consider this rude, maybe think the students should stop when an adult speaks. Nope, welcome to the 21st century. Verbs keep acting. They do. They come. And just as quickly, they go. After all, the bell just rang, lockers are slamming, the clock is ticking, teachers or coaches are waiting. Time to move. All-ways, it's time to get somewhere.

"How'd you guys sleep last night?" I ask generally to the two or three who are awake. I'm halfway not even expecting an answer. The conscious few appear ready to go off into iPod land. I want to gauge the mood if you catch my drift.

Bryn, Molly Niepoky and Grace Brock look up. They smile. They're all teeth when they do this. Their whole faces get into the act and I could almost swear they glow. Personally, I'm not a father but you're not human if you don't find this... adorable. I want to stop the van and pinch those cheeks when they smile that way. It gives me comfort, makes me know there is good in the world and in our young.

In fact, to digress for a second, it's these little things that make me the one who often stops in the halls. It's after they said something perhaps inappropriate, or did something, or maybe even threw something. Sure, I'm supposed to correct, but I mostly find it so spontaneous. Often I'm jealous because I want to hold on to that and I'm not real sure I know how, or if I'm even capable at my age.

My own mind cranks into hyper mode when Bryn is the one who answers, "I slept like a rock!" This too is highly unusual the night before game day. A good night's sleep before a big game is usually unheard of. Thoughts gather, wait in line while scenarios are played out , good and bad. Each thought waits to enter, ready to dive in like kids into a pool on the first day of summer.

Still, that's her answer. She smiles again when she says it; my three conscious girls consider our conversation over and go into iPod world.

I just drive. Forty-two miles to go and ninety-two minutes to do it in. As of this very moment, life is good.

We park somewhere in the middle of a field, wait in line while the parking attendant points to plot T somewhere between the biggest, longest buses ever. Great chance of getting blocked in but I'm not worried about that now.

As the kids gather their belongings and get out, my brain is playing through scenarios of my own. I have 65 young 'uns to look after today and I'll do it, but I've made up my mind to be as good as I can be today as a coach. If kids can have their Vision Quests, darn it, I can too.

They grab pillows and blankets and iPods and phones, book bags, athletic bags, spikes and even teddy bears. Some still have mattress marks on their little faces. Many seem a little ticked off about this early morning Saturday thing. The veterans are used to it, they'll be laughing with each other before we even get the tent put up. Eventually the sleepers will follow suit.

They will pick out the best spots on the tarp. Some will go back to sleep. Others will clamor around, looking for someone to poke or prod. Bryn usually plugs into her phone and closes her eyes. "I always pretend to be asleep but I'm not," she once told me.

For now though, she and Molly are playing tug-of-war with a phone cord. Neither have found their spaces yet so they're playfully taking it out on each other. Eventually Molly gets her cord back, takes off her shoes, rolls into her spot. Bryn finds her a place, tosses her pillow, follows suit.

All will get comfortable eventually, some even resting against one another. The serious ones will be nervous. The not-so-serious will perhaps wondering how they got into all this. Regardless, it's the calm before the storm and each, at some point, must think about what they're here for.

It's what happens.

Coach Jayaraj has them warm up approximately 50 minutes before show time. It's the beauty of preparation. The kids know what to do. They will run for around 10 minutes, do their dynamic stretches, and then make their last-minute adjustments to their spikes, their hair, or their clothes.

Bryn must pin her jersey on tighter; it's two sizes too big. I'm not sure if we ran out of the new ones or if she was too slow to get in the line. The uniforms are new and pretty and they stand out, but just like the old ones, hers is too big.

Still, the rituals and the nerves are all over the place now. I can feel it as I circle the tent. "Do you have an extra pin?" "Remember to tie your chip in tight!" "Tape up your shoes if you have to. Do we have any more tape?"

Words are starting to spill out at 500 words per minute with gusts up to 750. Little bodies are scurrying, hurrying. Now that I think about it, I'm even getting a little nervous myself.

At 12 minutes before, they begin the walk to the starting line. It's about 100-plus meters away. They must do their strides, huddle together in each other's' arms, talk about things. Like the smile thing, the huddle is something that makes me just stand

and watch. In fact, I often don't even wonder what they're saying; I feel it's something they and they alone deserve. No coaches, no parents, no lectures, let them work it out. What they say is none of my business, and I'm one of the coaches.

Eventually they un-arm themselves and sprint back. Then forth. Back. Forth.

Bryn and our team captain, Izzy, are talking. Izzy is our veteran; she usually gets quiet and doesn't like to be bothered. Bryn and she train together, though, so they have roots. In fact, last year they even joked about being each other's conscience. It's funny, but when you into running that actually makes sense in a funny, demented kind of way.

Regardless, the two heads come together at the front of the line. Bryn and Izzy discuss what they need to discuss and they both smile. They hug. They are ready.

The team bunches in together, adjusts their watches, wait impatiently while some race director goes through his spiel.

They've heard it before – most have anyway. At this late season point, they only want to hear one thing. Eventually, they do.

A starting gun goes off in Douglasville.

6:15 - Bryn goes through the mile right on schedule, but there is a problem, a big problem. It rained last night – hard – so she's already sloshed through a couple of puddles; almost slipped a time or two.

Her start was fast, but not (state champ) Serena Tripodi fast, as she was instructed. It's sort of the oxymoron of a race: you're told not to go out too fast, but if you don't get out pretty fast you get lost in the shuffle; boxed in with the field.

It's tricky, but you need to go out reasonably fast and then settle in fast, if that makes any sense. Lots of running things are tricky. For example, she was told all summer that she needed to train slower where she could race faster. If you're not a runner, that may make no sense. If you are, you get it.

In looking back, my summer runs with her were social but with that very point: You have to run at "Dunn' pace." Her eyes would roll but she would smile again, adjust her watch and off we would go. Just as often, there wasn't much conversation except for me telling her to slow down, to stay with me. She would laugh. "Oh, I forgot! We're running at Dunn pace!"

If we turned her loose, every jog would be a race. Her mind can do it but last year her shins could not. She was in a stress fracture boot by November. Again, it happens.

Our laughs would give way to our feet pounding away at the trail of the river. It was hot out, more reason to keep it slow. When you're older you get that too, though perhaps too late. Verbs, however, don't understand it yet.

Summer is only a memory for now though. The pools are all closed. It's October, decades have happened in a kid's life. And none of it matters. Except this. Now. It's time for the second mile.

13:04 - It's muddy and the sun has come out, neither conducive for achieving a Vision Quest. Still, Bryn's legs chug forward, Coach Jayaraj's voice still in her head. Jayaraj is a passionate man and Bryn a driven athlete. The two work together in a cohesive way, though Bryn - having the typical Type-A mentality of the distance runner, sometimes wonders if she's working hard enough. "The clock won't lie," Jayaraj always says. "I'd rather you run faster on Saturdays than on Tuesdays."

Bryn will acknowledge, accept, and (as she said to me after my Yoda text), eventually admit: "I believe you."

On she runs. She's tired and her heart is in it, but, as Jayaraj's voice fills her mind, the clock won't wait.

19:47 - Three miles are down, but now for the dreaded point-one. That's 185 yards for those of you scoring at home, and it can be the toughest thing there is.

Bryn rounds the corner and sees the finish, looks at her

watch, hears the crowd. She's sixth overall, more than great for a sophomore racing against bigger schools. Still, like the normal mindset of an achieving kid, this isn't enough. The clock is ticking...ticking... She doesn't think she'll make it.

Her heart sinks but her legs do not. She runs like she's trained to run. Those miles, those summer trails, those early morning jogs around the neighborhood, they're never for nothing.

Champions don't quit. They don't fail either, not for long. The clock passes 20:00 but she shrugs it off. She sprints for all she's worth and crosses the finish line. The clock reads 20:34. Briefly, she is sad, frustrated, wanting to scream.

Bryn looks down. She has 19:52 written on her hand; it's been written there daily for the last two months. Did she do something wrong? Did she train too hard? Not hard enough? Why didn't she make it?

She hears a voice. It's Izzy – she just came in right behind her. And there comes Kate...then Megan...then Evan...then Molly – on down the line to the 10th runner.

FINISH - They huddle again. Bryn is hugged by all teammates. They all know her, love her, respect her. She hasn't failed at anything. Izzy, the captain and the rock, tells her how good she did. Tells her she has nothing to be ashamed of and she "ran awesome!" Izzy did well herself, as did Kate, Megan, Evan, Molly...down the line again.

Deep down Bryn knows it, accepts it, believes it. She has come to trust, love and respect Ileana and her teammates the way she does the sport. Runners, like the clock, don't lie. You either put it all out there or you don't. Izzy and Bryn always do. All the younger teammates are starting to also.

It's simply one of the great things about sports that are hard to explain. Still, if you work hard, it's what happens.

I walk away from the huddle out of respect. It's their moment. Still, I look. Bryn is smiling now. They all are. Oh, so many cheeks I could pinch right now. And right about…now…I hear a camera go off.

Someone has photographed this moment in time, a time when ten cross country girls just put it on the line for perhaps 10 different reasons. Some wanted to break 20, some wanted to win the team trophy, some just wanted to finish to go off and enjoy their long weekends.

Still, they all did it. And on their faces shows achievement, sacrifice, guts, that "we did it" look on the faces of 10 hyperactive verbs. They look so happy, so spontaneous, so resilient.

No, verbs don't stay sad for long and these are rarely inactive. I will always see that moment. There's so much going on in the world, so much so right and so much so wrong. Regardless, I choose to see 10 kids simply unclasping, breaking out of a huddle.

My eyes are searching for the photographer.

I want a copy of that picture.

Essay update: Eventually, Bryn would go on to break the 20-minute barrier, at least twice if my memory serves. The first time was later that same season, in November, down at a course near Fairburn. No, it wasn't a 19:52 but a 19:54.4. Yes, the smile on her face was beyond priceless, the reason I do what I do.

Two years later, as a senior, she would top out at 19:27 at the Asics Invitational. Currently, she is on to UNC this fall. Though not on the team, she has no plans to stop running.

And Another Milestone...

Quite frankly, I can't decide if I love moments like this more as a coach, a journalist or a human being. Seeing kids set goals, write them down, visualize, train and go for it is one of the many reasons I love what I do.

With that said, my eyes are on Blake Morain on Cross Country Senior Night 2017 as our kids gather at the track after school. There is no fancy plot: He is trying to break the 5-minute mile; his best going in is a 5:01.8. I spent some time yesterday after practice with Blake as he prepared. No, I'm not taking, nor do I deserve, any credit. As an observer, I watched while he ran his laps. "I'm visualizing my splits for tomorrow," he said as he passed. I simply stood back while he crossed his imaginary finish line, checked his watch, walked off the track, stretched.

I have learned as a teacher, friend, or coach when it's best to simply shut up and get out of the way. No words needed, no advice, no coaching. Instead I offered a simple "good luck" as he walked by me, heading to the parking lot. He gave me a fist bump, and I could see by the look in his face that he was ready. I laughed to myself and almost said out loud, "You're not going to sleep tonight."

I kept it to myself as he walked off the track and to his car. My brain went back to two years ago when I kept close track of our beloved Bryn Foster in her attempt to break the 20-minute barrier in the 5K. Yes, I was there when she failed, and I was there when she did it. I still remember her smile when she saw that 19:54.4 glowing on her watch. Her face was beaming from left ear to right one, covering everything in between. I will always see that smile; when I don't feel like performing it will poke me in the ribs, keep me going. It even puts a mantra in my skull:

Believe in yourself.

Set your sights.

Persevere.

Go for it.

As for the present moment, Blake's problem is the weather. Though it was great this morning, 48 degrees at Eastern Golden Bear Car Pool Time, it has warmed to 80 over the hours. I always hate the running announcers when they say a 70 to 80-degree day is a "perfect day for running." It's not, a 70 to 80-degree day is a perfect day for the announcers – 40 to 50 is a perfect day for running.

Regardless, race time comes when race time comes. As Coach Jayaraj always says, "The show goes on; you can't call time-out." Heat or cold, rain or shine, there comes a time when there's nothing left to do but to do it. With that said, 14 runners walk onto the track, many still getting loose, others walking to the start as if going to a slaughter. Ready or not...

0:00 - Blake looks almost too pumped as he toes the line. For a second I think I'm going to get a look at his lunch. Sorry, but when you coach this sport, it happens. It's who we are, what we do, often we'll even brag about it later. Still, he kicks his legs, checks his watch, adjusts his shorts. I click on my own watch, praying I'll get to stop it less than five minutes later.

A gun fires and off they go.

1:10 – Houston we may have a problem. Blake is running astride junior teammate Porter Null. Porter's going for a 4:48. Blake going out that fast, combined with the heat, could be a dream-ending mistake. Still, he looks reasonably comfortable as he closes out his first quarter. The gathering people cheer in full support, holler encouragement as he goes past. Blake stares ahead, in rhythm, good cadence. Still, a 70-second quarter is awful fast. Most people run PRs in the mile on even or negative splits.

2:29 – Porter has left him, a good thing in this coach's mind. Blake is with teammate Nick Gonzalez and he's right on target now, not a second to waste. He looks okay but man, it's hot. It seems late October would bring us cooler temperatures, though God appears to have other plans. Still, Blake runs on. Some members of the crowd get out of their seats and head toward the infield. Enthusiasm is contagious; there's energy all around us.

3:47 – One lap to go and he's two seconds slow. My heart drops. Can he possibly make up this time in this heat? As he jogs by my mind takes off. After all, this coach/journalist is appreciating what he's seeing, heads or tails. You see, in distance running it's between you and you. You race in remote fields somewhere in towns with no red lights. Maybe you'll get a moo out of cow; if it's early enough you can hope to spot a deer. As for motivation, you must dig deep, there's simply no other way.

That's why this sport attracts such good kids. The pain and the sheer toughness creates a bond. In other sports, you might beat someone badly and feel nothing but superiority over them. With running, regardless of the pace, there is an appreciation, a glue, a fraternity that's fun to talk about as soon as you're inside the chute. Win? Lose? You both endured, felt pain, kept going anyway. You don't know each other's names but you're friends.

For now, Blake Morain has a luxury, aa luxury often not afforded a distance runner. He has noise, full support, screaming classmates, teammates, teachers and people simply wanting to know what's going on. Unlike on cross country courses, though, he's not leaving your sight and running off in the woods. What will or won't happen is out in the open; he'll make it or he won't – and either way it will happen in full view.

And it is already being talked about before he even finishes the sacred lap number four.

"I still had confidence I could do it," he would later say. "I knew it wasn't over till I crossed the finish line."

With 300 meters to go, he kicks the gear up to 90 percent, thermometer be darned. With 200 to go, it's all or nothing. This is what he's visualized for; this is his dream; this is why he didn't sleep last night. This is it.

At the 100-meter mark it's a sprint, or it's all the sprint he's got. Porter has already crossed, as has Nick. Blake kicks his arms, lifts his knees and, races for all he's worth. As he crosses the finish line he lets out a loud scream.

And it's a scream of joy…he crossed in 4:57.

Finish line - The runners are now all huddled together, high-fiving, gabbing, chattering. Adrenaline everywhere. As a writer, I have questions but then I think again. As I noted earlier, sometimes knowing when to shut up is more important than knowing what to say. I often preach that if you can use common sense, you don't have to think. This is particularly true in coaching, but also in writing, teaching, life its own self.

I look around at all this, at this sport, these people, this sweat, this scene. A good portion of our school is down here. They are chattering the way kids do, gesturing, comparing times, laughing. Coach Jayaraj is restarting his watch ready for the next race. The starter is grabbing his gun. Blake is surrounded and he's all smiles.

"I'm happy with what I did, but I'm already trying to beat this time in my head," Blake says as he walks up. The coaches all smile, nobody corrects this mindset and no one should. Instead, he gets a pat on the shoulder, one type-A mindset talking to another. "At least try to enjoy it," a coach says.

Blake smiles, shakes all our hands. He's classy that way, in every way now that I mention it. He'd shake our hands if he didn't make it. He'd simply set another goal if the clock had read 5:01. That's who he is, that's why our job working with him is so easy. We all just stand and watch while he trots to catch up with his teammates and head back to his car.

Things are winding down now and, you know, you have to appreciate times like this, no running pun intended. A friend used to call it a pure moment. My roles as coach and journalist for today are over. I've seen something I live for; there's no-where else I'd want to be...and around no other people. Most of what I love is right before me.

I now stand at the finish line filled with gratitude. A senior to die for just gave it all he had on Senior Night, put it on the line for all to see. He would have succeeded whether he made it or not, if that makes any sense. It feels good just being around it.. There's no more conversation or questions needed. What just happened will speak for itself.

Instead, I simply reset my watch back to zero, walk off the track. Staring at the race clock one last time, I walk back to my car and I smile.

A Gift from the Universe

This is what happened:

I just finished reading "Thank & Grow Rich" by Pam Grout, a great book on gratitude I totally recommend. In it, she made the comment, and I'm paraphrasing here, that upon reading this book you will soon receive a physical gift from the Universe – a sign if you will. This registered within me. For at least a year now, I have been trying to find some type of symbol that represents sacredness for me.

So far, no such luck.

On a connecting note, I have had rocks on my brain for the past two months. If you know me, you have no problem believing this. The reason is that our cross country kids, the girls anyway, have a cute little ritual that consists of running into the woods, grabbing a big rock, and then placing it on this sewer cover before running on. I think Ileana Zeissner started this; sounds just like her.

Also, and in connecting further, I've been thinking of writing a story about this ritual since I've already done one about another custom the girls have of picking a leaf off a tree, dropping it over a bridge at the river, and then watching the leaf as it goes down into the water. If you see the leaf all the way down, your wish will come true. If you don't, it won't.

Anyway, early last week I had the morning off so I chose, not only to go to the river, but also to run to the rock pile to see if I could find my sign. Yes, I know, you're not supposed to force such things, but I wanted the opportunity to see one that reached out and grabbed me, one I could touch every day before heading out the door, one that would give me goosebumps.

Off I went. It was a beautiful morning and I was probably going faster than normal, first because of the weather and second, because of my quest. I took my left past the bridge, went left again on what I call "Molly's Trail" (named after the wonderful Molly Niepoky) and into the woods I went.

I got to the rock pile. I looked. There were a couple of cute rocks. Nice. Eye-catching. But nothing jumped out at me. Nothing that made me think, "I AM YOUR SIGN FROM THE UNIVERSE!" I was disappointed, I SO wanted my sign to be one of these rocks that connects me with my school and, furthermore, to my cross country kids.

Still, we move on. In keeping with tradition, I picked up what I thought was the cutest rock, put it on top of the concrete shelf and I kept going. Life goes on, things happen, keep moving forward.

Out of the woods I ran still enjoying the day, still trying to practice my gratitude I learned about in the book. At the same time, however, I was a bit disappointed. Where was my sign? I want my gift? Where is my symbol of peace?

The run neared its end. I always stop at the same place I start – right by where the Holy Innocents' kids do their stretching at what we call "The Stretching Hole." On this day, however, I decided to change it up a bit. I have a desire not to turn into Sheldon Cooper on *The Big Bang Theory*; I don't want every second of my life to be structured, so instead of the usual stretching on one of those two picnic tables, I decided to walk further to the second to the last table before you get back to the parking lot – right there by the 5K pole.

So, I'm walking, life is good. I'm healthy, reasonably sane and

I've come SO far from where I was 10 years ago when I was clinically depressed and living life as a "people person with no people." When you get down to it, I have no complaints whatsoever.

I'm almost at the picnic table, almost at the 5K pole, when it happened. Right there, sitting ON TOP of the 5K pole, was a huge rock, I mean a 30-pound, have-to-carry- with-two-hands, boulder of a rock, sitting right there.

Now, I've been running at the river for 20-plus years and I have NEVER seen a huge rock sitting on top of ANY mile marker. In fact, to prove I wasn't forcing this, some walkers looked over and said, "What is that rock doing sitting on top of that pole? Must be a candid camera under there," one of them joked. "If you pick up the rock you'll be on camera!"

Ha-ha.

I stretched and I laughed. There it was, my sign, my rock, my symbol at last. I waited until the walkers moved on; didn't want anyone to see me lifting this heavy thing and stowing it into my car. They walked on; I finished my stretch; I grabbed the rock and I stowed it into my car.

The heck of it is, it fits on my table normally. If you walked in, it wouldn't jump out at you. You wouldn't say what those walkers said. "What in the heck is that rock doing sitting on your table?" It matches the color of the jigsaw puzzle it rests upon. I placed a necklace over it, made a shrine out of it. It blends. It fits. It is.

I woke up the next morning with 500 words per minute going through my head. My meditation was horrible. My mind was a cesspool. Then I saw my rock and I laughed.

It's all going to be okay...

Spring and the Smiles That Come With it

Maybe it's because I don't have to wipe the frost off my nose anymore after coming in from carpool. Or wake up 30 minutes earlier to get the ice off my windshield. Could be because we've got two or three hours more of daylight. I'll no longer glance at my watch and see it's 7:30 when it feels like midnight.

I hear baseballs cracking after school now, starting guns firing at tracks, tennis coaches are grabbing their kids at the changeovers, and even the soccer and lacrosse coaches during night games are peeling off their four layers.

Spring. Prom. Growing grass. Count downs to graduation. Eating outside. Walking the dog and not being in a hurry to get back. It's putting your coats away and hoping this isn't a repeat of 1993, when we were teased with spring only to get hit with 6 unwelcome inches. (Fifteen years later, people still talk about that. I'm over it. So is Mother Nature. I hope.)

My 524 kids are strewn across beaches as I write this, from Punta Cana to the Dominican to Belize to Florida. I'm feeding off their energy while typing in St. Simons – my mind shuffling through my former beach misdeeds. Don't judge me out there, most of you were right beside me. That's why I love you; that's why we're bonded no matter where our bodies are.

It's Little League baseball where my mind goes. Mom and

Dad bought me my glove; brother Chip taught me how to put oil in it and wrap it in a belt to break it in. An obedient soul, I oiled and wrapped; yet Chip never taught me all this wouldn't help me catch the ball. Wasn't that included in the price?

To this day I cringe at a game when my team is up by a run in the last inning, two outs, but the tying and winning runs are on second and third. A very large left-handed batter hit a towering fly ball into that Madison, Ga. sky that night. The second baseman (me), stared hopelessly up at it, my heart dropping as I realized I was the one supposed to catch it.

The runners were off at the crack of the bat; both had touched the plate right as the ball never touched my freshly-oiled glove. We lose. Season over. Angry coaches. Mom and Dad dreading the ride home with their loveable goat crying in the back seat.

Knowing my mom, she probably thought it was cute. Dad simply crossed "baseball scholarship" off the possibilities for Baby Dunn. I would move on to Berry and to tennis – where the racket was much bigger, the ball softer, and the practices co-ed. Brat, maybe, but I've got a little sense. Besides, I never did look good in baseball baggies.

True, Spring Break ended for most of you once you took your first real job. And yes, I hear all my friends who call me a Peter Pan, wonder when I'll ever grow up. I have a good answer for the growing up thing. You see, I made the mistake of catching the news this morning. I watched grown-ups in action; saw all the anger.

Frankly, I'm still not that impressed. I'll settle for slamming lockers, ringing bells, kids flirting, Prom, Winterfest, Homecoming, all this keeps me sharp with the turning of the four seasons.

Spring Break or no, young or old, I'm sending peace to you all, even if you did lose the game for your team one beautiful spring night; missed the front end of a 1-and-1; got rejected on

Prom night. Good for you. Feel the fear and have the guts to keep living anyway. Damn the torpedoes. Set the sights. Aim high. Keep shooting. Call her. Go for it. Winter's gone.

And, as I once read, comfort zones are simply beautiful. Problem is, nothing ever grows there.

Miracles
Happen...Believe it

It's always fun to read about miracles. It gives you that warm feeling, motivates you, perhaps makes a tear or two drop out of your eyes. It's even better, however, when it happens right in front of your face.

HIES senior Alex Thomas, before his junior year, cut his hand open. Bad. The cut went through nine tendons, two nerves and one artery. "If I hadn't gotten immediate attention, I would've bled out," he later said.

The doctors told him he'd probably never use his right hand again. Pole vaulting would be beyond a miracle. He'd have to learn to adjust. This would be bad news for anyone. When you're in high school, however, you're an active verb; you come, you go, you do things. Alex, also a running back and cornerback on the football team at the time, is also a painter. In his spare time, if there is any, he works on cars. In short, both hands often required.

For Alex, the doctor's news wasn't a death sentence. Instead, using his own words, it was "game on." He went to work. Curling exercises, in the weight room and off to rehab were the norm, while, in the meantime, he learned to be ambidextrous; practiced writing and painting with his left hand. Besides pole vaulting, you see, Alex has his artistic dreams. "I like Picasso, but I want to create my own style."

His work outside of rehab eventually became so intense, he eventually quit going. He was doing enough. Soon, he could hold a pole. Not win a meet, mind you, but simply hold a pole. Perhaps equal or more importantly, he believed.

After having to sit out football season, he came to track in January actually ahead of the game. He was vaulting again, using his hand, writing, painting. "It still hurts to this day, though it doesn't impede my day-to-day activities," he said.

And it didn't last spring. Starting semi-slowly in the vault, he got better...and better. At the state meet at Berry College last May, he won the state championship with a vault of 13 feet, 6 inches. His best during the season was 14 feet.

A year later, people are asking him about the possibilities of repeating as state champion. He's set to go to Savannah College of Art & Design in Savannah this fall to pursue his art dream, regardless, but people tend to gravitate toward sports in one way or the other. Can he do it? Is there pressure? How cool was it when he won state? Did he have it engraved and hang it on his wall?

He didn't hesitate answering any of the questions when he responded, "You know, I'm just out to do the best I can. If I win state, I win state. As for winning last year, I got a medal, it was just a medal. In fact, I eventually gave it to my physical therapist."

Yeah, still loving our kids...

Essay update: Alex did repeat as state champion. He vaulted a personal best 15 feet and just missed the Class A–Private meet record by an inch. "Ever since I won state last year I wanted the meet record," he said afterwards. "I already had a state title; I wanted to go for it all. Still, it's a great way to go out."

When asked if he gave this medal away, he responded with a laugh. "No, I think I'm going to keep this one."

Running Camp? What in the Hell is That?

In three weeks, I'm off to running camp in Asheville, NC. The first time I told one of my students I was doing this, he quickly replied, "Running and camp are two words that should NEVER be used in the same sentence."

Another common response: "You're going to what? Running? Camp?"

That's what I thought. Still, I'm weird, so in 2004, while still disguised as a married man, I signed up. In retrospect, the wife might have helped me out of the house, but that's another story. Still, I made the LONG drive from West Palm to Asheville. Spent a week up there.

Haven't been the same since.

Distance runners, I have found, are a different breed. It's a group where the pain and suffering creates a thick bond, makes you friends. It's kind of like, "Wow, you're as demented as I am! What's your name?" Yeah, something like that.

In Asheville, I enter every summer a time warp. Hundreds of us simply call a time-out on life – I highly recommend this – and we head up into the mountains. On Friday, we actually run up one – it's called Buzzard Bait. I remember trying to impress my peers at the starting line on that 2004 day.

"I feel like a million bucks," I said. My friend laughed.

"That's great," he said. "Problem is, it takes three million to get to the top."

He was right. Damn him.

I commiserated about my divorce in Asheville, found out I did and didn't have prostate cancer. My roommate last summer learned his wife was pregnant. (He flew out the third-floor window upon hearing the news, but also, another story.) I've coached my kids to both first, and last-place finishes, in the pacing contest. Came close to getting struck by lightning and dying there.

It's an adventure on steroids, where the very campers and staff who work you up are the same ones who help you through it. Strange, but there it is…

As for Asheville, it's the Berkeley of the South, a place where locals, hippies and tourists all share the same soil. Somehow, it all works. You can find anything up there, except a parking place. And the music and the food and the beer – and the people I've met – are priceless.

We go there to share this thing called distance running. Fifteen of my kids will be with me this July. I'm an observer of the game. I like to watch and hear them as they go through the week. It's a rollercoaster for them; the catch is they'll get off at a totally different place from where they got on.

I write this because camp of any kind keeps you young; gives you the time-out you deserve. We're pounded with info and jobs and chores and information and comparisons. Mental health is a serious issue. Me, I'm a selfish soul, probably take more "me" time than I should. I'm an experienced camp goer; 20 years ago, I went to an eight-week camp in New Hampshire. All I wanted was a part-time job, I came home with a wife.

I looked on the sign-up sheet when I got home and didn't find a word on there about that anywhere. Still, I digress once again.

I'm ready for my time-out and to move forward, though I know how weird that sounds. And perhaps as I pen these words, my own mental health should be called to question. After all, in three weeks I'm going to run up a friggin mountain.

And I can't wait to do it.

Meditations from a Feel-Good Friday

It's all consciousness and energy, everything else is outer shells and God's details. I say this because I'm fortunately swept up in the feel of my school while standing at carpool.

To bring you the picture: It's not a normal day. The football players are in their jerseys – they have a spring game next week. The baseball players are heroes; they're off to the Final Four after winning their rubber game yesterday. The track state championships are today and tomorrow at Berry College. And the golfers have state coming up, also proud after winning area for the second straight year.

As for the seniors, it's their last day of class, which means there is no class. Which means Frisbees and frolics and music and Hawaiian shirts and this game called Spike Ball, something they've been doing since out of the womb. Not sure of the rules, but it requires a lot of yelling and movement and confusion, which is perfect for these random events waiting to happen, also known as active verbs, also known as students.

I laugh at their outfits, feel their senioritis from head to toe; envy their future and this four-year adventure in non-reality known as college. I remember my dad - as brother Chip often recalls - leaning against his shovel while saying, "I envy you boys," when we were headed off.

I'm surrounded by energetic heroes. And it's Friday and the weather's nice. And I'm realizing things can be this good often if you just let the energy in, which often requires removing head from backside. Breathe in, look within, but get out of yourself. Enjoy this. This God we talk about has many definitions, gets a lot of credit and takes way too much blame. I'm here to simply insist He is a creative genius. We make the mistake of watching the news and questioning, but there's perfection here, a perfect order among the disorder if you will.

I must finish now because I'm off to find Will Rautenstrauch, a quiet junior I once coached. We've never had any connection; we simply pass in the halls. Young Will, in probably his first at-bat in his high school life yesterday, delivered a huge 2-run single to left on a 3-2 count. Helped win us the game.

I'm not off to form a pseudo-friendship; not off to force anything. I just want more energy and to see his; want to see the look in his face when he's hugged and congratulated. Why, because of what Robin Williams said in the movie Dead Poets Society.

"Quite simply, these are the things we stay alive for."

For the Love of Pets

He would lift his back leg and pee on his front one. For nine years, this made me laugh every morning, rain, shine, or all three times during hurricanes. One day, while sitting in my rapidly-getting-empty condo due to my divorce, I sat alone on the stairwell, just me and my pity.

I heard him before I saw him, he had that bell stuck on his collar. Get the picture: I'm on my butt, hands draped across both knees – staring out into nowhere. Jasper trots up the stairs, anchors down his two back legs, looks up at me.

Sorry naysayers, but sometimes you can read minds, and perhaps dogs more than people. He told me this: We don't have a pot to pee in, but I'll always love you. What's next? Wherever we go, whatever we do, I'm with you.

Not being a father, I'm quite sure nothing can match that of the parent's love for their own. Still, I can't help but think that the unconditional love we get from pets has to rank right up there somewhere. Even today, when the moon is tilting funny; when the traffic lights are all red, and the words won't rhyme – I see Jasper looking up at me on that stairwell.

In short, I'm good at being humbled. After all, I've been in a marriage and I've run marathons. In contrast to people that gripe about one or the other, I love the fairness of it. After all, it doesn't matter who you are, what you do, or how much money you make – take out the damn trash! Keep running! Both cases, there's work to be done, resumes be damned. Looks, charm or lack thereof are all out the window.

I'm running at the river as these words are popping into my head. It hasn't been a particularly productive day, nor have I made my deceased parents proud for anything I've done. Yet, I'll keep running; keep moving forward.

After all, I want to be the kind of person Jasper always thought I was.

The Luxury of Hitting Rock Bottom

Marianne Williamson once wrote: "Sometimes you don't need to be deprived of hitting rock bottom." Janis Joplin sang, "Freedom's just another word for nothing left to lose."

Hitting rock bottom, I remember it well. I was walking Jasper and I knew I was in trouble when he did his peeing thing and I didn't think it was funny. About the same time, Bill Withers' voice came through my iPod singing, *"Ain't No Sunshine When She's Gone."*

May I never reach a lower moment than that Sunday afternoon in 2006, surrounded by palm trees, whirlpools and a beach less than three tenths of a mile away. Still, that day turned out, however ironically this may sound, to be one of the best days of my life.

Sometimes being strong is the only option you have. No talking. No reading. No lunch with friends. It's balls-to-the-wall, suck-it-up-and-go and hang in there for dear life. Sometimes you must be like the football teams every weekend – there's a sign in front of you and you simply run right through it. (Or as Jim Morrison sang: Break on through to the other side.)

That was my theme song for a year, and I wasn't even a Jim Morrison fan.

The beauty of that day is that fear left my life. It was time to do something even if it was wrong. I would make the call. Get in front of key people's faces. Tell them what I could and would do for them. Resumes, cover letters be damned. I drove nine hours one way – I'd do it again.

A John McEnroe interview before Wimbledon comes to mind. Love him or hate him, he tells it like it is. "Sometimes you just have to come out there with a kick ass attitude."

I would say may your backs never be to the wall, but they will be. I would say I hope you never get betrayed, but you will be. This is an ironic statement, but if you're floundering, maybe hitting rock bottom is the best luxury you'll ever have. May no one ever deprive you of that.

At the end of the day, sometimes it's simply between you and you. When the lights are red, my team is losing and I can't find anything but rap on the radio, I remember that day in Florida, when Bill Withers sang while my dog peed on his front leg.

I came back and you will, too. You weren't created to do anything else. Mother Teresa once wrote, "I know God will not give us any more than we can handle. I just wish that he didn't trust me so much."

Yeah, sometimes it's like that. New set of downs, move the chains, first and ten.

And God Bless.

Four Bullets and a Point

- Steve Prefontaine, if you believe the movie, was having a meltdown. Throwing off his shoes, he yelled to Coach Bowerman, "Nobody cares about the 5,000-meter run!" Bowerman quickly responded, "Well give them a reason to care!"
- Oscar Wilde was said to have written: "Be yourself, everyone else is taken." The first time I read this I laughed my butt off, but let's move on.
- I remember in seventh grade when they passed out our basketball jerseys. One of the older boys already had Pistol Pete's number, I got number 21. My dad heard me complaining about this when I got home. "It doesn't matter whose number you didn't get," he yelled. "Start your own thing. Down the road, people should be able to say they got YOUR number!"
- Finally, Dr. Seuss, an intelligent soul if there ever was one, wrote, "Today you are you, that is truer than true. Nobody can be more youer than you."

There it is, my morning essay. And even if you don't like Oscar Wilde, didn't follow running in the 70s or didn't know my dad, how in the world can anyone argue with Dr. Seuss? That just ain't right.

Getting Lucky

(Man, you people have dirty minds!)

You CAN declare yourself neither a Democrat nor a Republican. After all, some parts of both are great; others are batcrap crazy.

You CAN be a #16 seed and still beat a #1 seed. All it takes are belief and playing to win, instead of playing NOT to lose. I hope a lot of teams read that last sentence.

You CAN turn left at a yellow light. And I hope a lot of Atlantans read that one!

You CAN find your soul mate. But first, you must become your own.

You CAN shut up and walk away. You'll come out better anyway.

You CAN go back. Heck, I went to college twice and had a blast both times!

You CAN play free safety wearing Docksides, or a tiebreaker in your underwear. One warning, you might get arrested doing the last one. Damn, I miss the '70s and '80s.

You CAN play golf with your dad. I quadruple bogeyed every hole and loved every second of it.

You CAN question all the sayings. After all, absence makes the heart grow fonder isn't even accurate. And if you're loving the tunnel, who cares if there's light at the end of it or not?

You CAN do what you love. I never made above a B-minus

on a term paper and I failed the proficiency writing essay in school. Guess what I get paid to do?

You CAN get rejected twice in the same week while you're in college and remain classy. Okay, I couldn't, but I was young at the time...

You CAN be the luckiest person on the planet, if you choose to love your way through life instead of battling through it.

And finally, you can get lucky. Ironically, that's often accomplished by leaving her alone.

Grieving

I don't think you're ever supposed to stop grieving. Our biggest mistake is that we keep trying.

It's been about three years since Momma Shirley passed, went off to that big place in the sky where she could feed Muffin, clean up after Dad and basically be nice to everyone and everything that crossed her path. Funny thing, she did that while she was down here.

If you live long enough, you have been or will go through this. In all due respect to Mom and Dad, however, it's when the young ones go that's the worst. It defies the natural order of things; makes you mad at God. Me, I come from a small town that had basically one road to Athens: 441. We would all pile in cars and make that 25-mile drive for a lot of our teen-aged years. For us lucky ones, we always returned home, kissed our moms, went to bed. For others, the road twisted up and got them. Anger, tears and frustration followed.

I find the aftermath both painful times 12 and ironic. When we sit in pain and frustration and we're beside ourselves and it hurts so bad, that's the time when our passed on-loved ones are reaching out to us and telling us they're okay. I call it a "crap storm." Actually, I have another term for it but I'll be nice since people may be reading this.

It's ironic again that they send us signs and often we don't see them. We're too caught up in ourselves. Me, I sit now in my messy kitchen and laugh out loud. Dad would love this, he'd tell me I'm living right and pat me on the back. Mom would be simply appalled, she'd start cleaning immediately as there has NEVER been a room, a kitchen or a bathtub that she couldn't tidy up.

My old dog Jasper, who has also gone to that place in the sky, wouldn't have cared less. As long as he had a couch to groom himself on, all would be good. Walk him later, leave him alone, good night. Yes, contrasts are a beautiful thing. Somewhere along the line we wanted a ticket to the greatest show on Earth and we're getting it.

Still, I'm reminded of my mom and the one time she truly disciplined me. Yes, if you don't know already, I'm a spoiled brat though I don't blame anyone but myself. Anyway, I was 5 and I kicked sand in a kid's face at the beach. I thought and still think he deserved it, but Mom would have no part of me being mean. To anybody. At any time. She told me to apologize. I wouldn't. She insisted. At first, I wouldn't budge. I eventually did.

The lesson I learned: People can and will be jerks. As for you, you WILL be nice. Game. Set. Match. I think of her now when I want to tell somebody…you know.

I don't mean to be writing this as a downer, but I'm just like you are. Sometimes I sit alone and I miss them. My dad left the building 20 years ago. I still remember how bad his socks stank, how smart he was. I remember, as I've written, of how he told me to be my own self and start my own trends.

Oh, how I remember that. Because of his lesson, as flawed and as imperfect as I am, I will copy no one. For better and for worse. I will be me and I will die trying. And when I'm gone – as Rod Stewart so eloquently once sang, "when the sun goes low and you're home all alone, think of me and try not to laugh."

In moving on, we've all lost people. At Holy Innocents' we lost a beautiful, creative soul two years ago. She was 18 and headed for college and had the most radiant smile. Going back to childhood, being from Madison, Ga., death hits just as or even harder in a small town. We all know them, we JUST saw them, he was just HERE!

People react differently. I remember after my divorce people had the gall to give me a formula for how long it was supposed to take me to get over it. Seriously! A formula! For your emotions!

"You were with her 10 years; therefore, you're going to be depressed for five!" Someone said that to me with a straight face. "No!", another said. "It takes two years and don't make any major decisions until then." (For what it's worth, the major decisions part was correct.)

A good friend of mine simply looked me in the eye, told me to grow a pair and get back in the game. Still, I digress. After all, it's ALL-WAYS hard to get back on the proverbial horse when you're still in midair from falling. It just is. It takes time. How much time?

Well, let me sum it up this way: My dad passed on 20 years ago; my mom two. I've cried through two or three young ones at Holy Innocents', lost several Madison friends along the way and a few more in college. No, this isn't about me, I know you've probably lost as much or more.

Still, I keep coming back to this formula thing. After all, how long am I supposed to grieve? Do I take their age and divide it by...what? Do I calculate the years I knew them and put an X on my calendar when my grieving time is up? What date, might I ask, should I get back on the horse?

Just writing about formulas of any kind makes me a bit angry. When people give me that look after I've lost someone, they tilt their head a little and I know they mean well. And for the record, I am grateful that they care whether I'm over my divorce, or over the loss of my Dad or my Mom.

I just smile at this because I have my own formula, one I invite you to copy: No, I am not over it. A part of me will always grieve...and I will continue to try and turn grieving into love.

That's what my loved ones were and are. Therefore that's what I will do.

I Wish I Had Your Life...

I blame "Pistol" Pete Maravich, he's the one who started all this. He could take a basketball and do anything with it. Around and behind his back, through his legs, through his opponents' legs; he could shoot it off the fly, from coming around the pick. He was such a magician with a basketball that the radio announcer at the time, the late Skip Caray, had the hardest time describing what Pete would do when he drove into the lane.

He played in Atlanta for a while; I would lie in bed at night and listen on my earphones, even when the games were on the West Coast. I'd keep his stats, could almost swear I felt his laughter and his pain. When he won, I won. His loss was mine, too.

Oh, how I wanted to be Pistol Pete Maravich.

Middle school turned to high school, and one day I woke up a teenager. Life was full of classes, games, social awkwardness, and dances. Lockers slamming, kids flirting, stories spreading - true and untrue.

I would often sit on the sidelines and watch football practice; I'd take my place on game night on the sidelines and keep the stats. Would watch those big boys go at it, their bravery and their guts and their blood and their sweat. I would watch them walk the halls and get all the girls. On road trips, the football players sat in the back because that's where all the cool people sat. Me, if I'd been any closer to the front I'd have been driving but that's beside the point. While on trips, I'd often look back there; see the guys talking so effortlessly, making their jokes, wooing their women, displaying their charm.

Pep rallies happened and they happened often. The players' names would be called out and all those pretty cheerleaders would cheer and jump and smile. I'd stand off to the side and I'd watch all this – wondering why God made me 5-foot-6 and only 120 pounds, and with the physical aggression of an un-held blocking dummy.

Oh, how I wanted to be a football player.

A few graduations later, it was my turn and I was off to college. A new world: older women, more competition on the tennis court, different people in an unfamiliar environment. I sat in class, unfortunately not taking notes, and I watched how easily the professors delivered their lectures. Most no notes. They simply walked the floor, played with the chalk, strolled down the aisles. They recited names, dates, facts, figures, battles, you name it. They were so smart; all this seemed to come so easy.

Between classes I would watch those professors standing or sitting in the quad. Students would come up and vie for attention. They seemed to be Pied Pipers, those professors. Wherever they went a band of students followed. I remember one of my favorite things ever in this lifetime to do, besides making a pretty girl laugh, was to get time with one my teachers, and get in as deep a conversation as my narrow mind could go.

They seemed so happy, so easygoing, so natural, they in their tweed jackets and their khaki pants and their ties.

Oh, how I wanted to be a college professor.

Years later, I was out of college - graduated without honors - and I'm in my one-bedroom apartment I share with three people and I'm watching *Friends*. This Chandler Bing character on there is SO funny. He's got a comeback for everything, his timing is perfect, his jokes make me laugh out loud as I sit on my Goodwill bought sofa.

Chandler Bing makes $1 million per episode and gets to flirt on set with Courteney Cox and Jennifer Aniston. A movie set is his oyster. He owns every scene. As far as I can surmise, he lives well; probably pays more in taxes than I've made in my life.

Oh, how I wanted to be Chandler Bing.

It's present-day now and I'm sitting in shorts, a T-shirt and a hat, visiting with Skip Johnson, a tennis partner-become-friend whom I've known since 1975. We're on the outskirts of the Governor's Mansion, private schools, $10-million dollar homes, and we're about as natural as the Coral Reefer Band without Jimmy Buffett.

My mind takes off as it always does, and I think back to life. I'm surrounded by good people now and always have been - from my roots in Madison, Ga., to college at Berry, over to the Atlanta area. I've a job I can't wait to go to, and though I'm not the most physically brave human being alive, there ain't many kids at my school I wouldn't stand up and take a bullet for.

Yes, kids nowadays take a beating sometimes. Come meet ours. There are stories I could put on Facebook that would bring tears to your eyes. Mine, too. The best part about these stories? They're true. Every damn one of them. And in most cases the teachers had nothing to do with it. Good deeds, instigated by good deeds, producing more good deeds. I smile every day; I'm glad I know these kids. When I can, I stop them in the hallways just for a simple 22-second conversation. The kids are busy, they can't talk long, but I've learned to live for those conversations.

About this time a fancy car goes by breaking me out of my reverie. The driver clicks his remote and the gates open to his mansion. His place seems ornate times 12; he probably spent more money on that thing than I've made in all my life combined. My mind follows his car as he pulls in. My thoughts are drawn to him for a second and then I stop.

Not this time big guy.

I think I'll just be happy being me.

171

Just One Word... (but it needs to be said)

Now is as good a time as any. After all, one of the great things about getting older is you start to realize that if you have strong feelings for something or someone, it's time to voice them. If not now, when?

I think back 11 years when I was five figures in debt, pathetically sad over a lost wife and life, and a future that perhaps consisted of ripping tickets in half at the Tilt-A-Whirl.

Now it goes like this: I don't know how, but of all the people down here on this planet, I get to be the luckiest one. I feel guilty; it's not fair. I've been all things unholy times 743, and the number just keeps on rising.

I get paid to come to school every day and stand among our youth – help them cross the street, give out assignments in class, work with runners on the track or at the river. I watch them laugh and cry and slam lockers; make up and break up, take tests; play sports and go on road trips; spring break, Prom, Winterfest and Homecoming. I feel their energy in Senior Commons, admire their talents, marvel at the depth of the talent while listening to them sing.

One day I saw one crying in the hall. I plopped down and cried right with them. I still don't know why, maybe I just enjoyed the connection. Daily, I stand among fellow coaches and teachers and feed off their passion. You know, people are attracted to passion and they should be. It means you're around people who have had the guts to decide, to commit, to make a life while on this planet.

A lot of people at where I work are like that. This is why I wake up every morning before my alarm clock goes off. This is why I keep showing up. Life rewards that, you know? Sometimes you don't have to do much special. You just show up and surround yourself with life and love and passion; plays and music and kids who flirt and cram for tests, talk at 750 words per minute, and walk the halls. People who take care of each other no matter what.

Private school brats? I've never met more well-rounded, caring people. I've never felt so appreciated. On days off, many leave this place and a part of me understands that. We all need to regroup, rewind, recharge and have well-rounded lives.

I'm not like that. I come here. Out there makes no sense to me. All I hear about are corrupt politicians, murders, snipers shooting people and nobody understanding why.

I look nowhere else. Don't need to. As I look back on this year, I'll have the exact comments I've had from 2007 on: I'm surrounded by everything I could ever want or need. Santa owes me nothing. Nor does life.

I close by offering the one word I'd give regardless of who I were talking to. I'd say it to God Himself if he were standing in front of me. Now I'll hereby say it unto you:

Thanks...

An Ode to Meditation

It's been one year now; every day, seven days a week. It started with 10 minutes but I shortened it to seven due to my short attention span. Also, I can hold seven minutes a LOT better than 10. You must go with what works – you must live your truth. The books will suggest how long you should do it. Don't listen. This is you. They don't know.

A few things stand out. First, the only BAD meditation is the one you don't show up for. It's like running: If you got out there and do it, then good for you. If your thoughts were bad while running, the fact that you even ran helped you get rid of them! Same with meditating. Sometimes your thoughts take off, and I mean take off. Let them go. If you weren't meditating, they'd be stuck with you throughout the day. Running and meditating will always hold parallels with me.

Second, I quit judging myself. Now after a seven-minute session, I feel that even if I only got 30 seconds of good breathing in, then that rocks! I used to judge that, compare it with the seven minutes, do the math and then think, "That sucked!" I was wrong. One simple breath can make the difference.

When I go under, my thoughts are that I'm breathing with God. My mind takes off and I'll think, "Enough. Take a couple breaths with God now." And I do. And my mind takes off again, and I remind myself to breathe with God. Sometimes I must go through plenty of repetitions. So be it. Don't judge it; keep going.

In moving on, the benefits of meditation help you vibrate at a better frequency. Therefore, you attract the good vibrations of people you encounter throughout the day. This has led me to great joy in interacting with my kids at school, watching them all giggling and laughing and being animated and spontaneous. I feel meditation has made me a magnet for that, I now walk the halls looking for people to talk to, searching for great spirits, lively conversations, the beauty and simplicity of small talk. It's who I am; it's what I do.

Finally, habits aren't that hard to form. After the first couple weeks, it becomes a part of your life. There were a few days I had to catch myself and say, "Oops, you almost forgot your seven minutes." Now, it doesn't happen. I allot that in my wakeup time. I'm glad. It helps. I look forward to future attractions.

I must go now. The bell just rang. People are out there. Can't wait...

Quotes That Won't Quit

"Remember, you are unique…just like everyone else." – Bumper sticker

"Am I drunk or is it me?" I was asked this once and I'm still not sure how to answer.

"I spent my earlier days looking for Mr. Right Now, instead of Mr. Right. Unfortunately, there's a very big difference." – a testimony given to me at a summer camp

"The only requirement for a perfect day is to have a happy mind." – Pam Grout's blog (I think)

"When a web is begun, God sends thread." – inscribed on the ceiling of the Library of Congress

"If you can keep your mind clear from unnecessary things, this could be the best day of your life." – Phil Jackson's book Sacred Hoops

"I don't know if I made the right decision or not, but I do know I won't have to make another one for four more years." Mark Davey, after joining the Army

"Coach, I'm only cheating myself and, if I can deal with it, then you should be able to." – Tennis player after I caught him cheating on his wind sprints.

"What do you want me to be – a prude, a tease or a slut?" – I was asked this on a date once

"I'm going to come to the net after every ball – you pass me 48 times, the match is yours." – Peter Howell, when introducing himself to his opponent before a singles match.

"Fat, drunk and stupid is no way to go through life, son." – *Animal House*

"Fat is in!" – Angie Hickman before eating her fourth bowl of soup

"Anyone can be nice when things are going well – even serial killers can do that! When things are tough, then what do you got?" – Mr. Jack Purcell

"Of course I'm late! If I could be on time I wouldn't be looking for a job." – Mark Davey again, this time after being chastised for being late for a job interview

"The mosquitos are so big here they need to be cleared for landing." – Mike Piazza during spring training down in Florida

"Somebody's Oh has got to go!" Don King – before two unbeaten boxers stepped into the ring.

"Your faith has saved you. Go in peace." – The Bible

"When the game is over, the king and the pawn go back into the same box." – A Proverb

"Why is it that the guy that's telling me to calm down is usually the same guy that ticked me off in the first place." – Roy Benson

Peace, love and Elvis

Reasons to Stay Alive

Today is my 58th birthday. My gift to myself are these 58 reasons for staying alive – mainly because 12 years ago today I couldn't even think of one. Sometimes we need reminding. Today, I'm reminding myself…

- Leaving work on a Friday, with a weekend agenda filled with nothing.
- Game 7, any sport
- The first sip of vanilla coffee in the morning
- A pencil in hand and a crossword puzzle daring me to fill in the blanks
- Hearing my XC kids chattering on the bus when driving them to the river
- A hot bath, even though that may not be considered manly
- October in Georgia
- Running at the river; God meets me there and I can hear Him
- Hitting "send" on a good day, not hitting it on a bad one
- Sitting in hot tubs, no reason needed
- A couch, a blanket, and a good book.
- Enjoying the challenge of writing a speech or an essay

- Gratefulness of returning to Atlanta; beating a depression
- Hearing that strange laugh my girlfriend has – a guffaw on steroids
- An old episode *of The Wonder Years* – Kevin was a mess, but Winnie was adorable
- 80s movies – because *Caddyshack, Ridgemont High, Fletch,* and *Stripes* are hard to beat
- "Be True to Your School" by Bob Greene – It's a diary of 1964 – nostalgic nirvana
- Writing up Friday night football with a glass of red wine
- The energy at a high school, any day, every day
- Hearing the starting gun go off at a cross country race – even more energy
- The smell of bubble gum – because I'm weird
- Having the discipline to only have two
- Putting on a long-sleeved T-shirt
- The Traveling Wilburys, a massive, mixture of talent
- Feeling the fear and doing it anyway; almost a daily occurrence with me
- Naps, the most underrated thing ever besides water and remote controls
- The Comedy Channel, because laughter is underrated, too
- Mom and Dad's voices inside my head – their bodies have passed, but they have not.
- Holy Innocents' Episcopal School, enough said
- Random 22-second conversations in the halls with kids between classes
- Doing nothing, rebelling against a society that keeps insisting you do something.

- Reconnecting on Facebook. My girlfriend is living proof this is a good thing.
- Smoothies, any kind, from any place, any time, anywhere.
- A gin & tonic buzz on an odd Saturday.
- Speaking at athletic banquets to my young 'uns.
- Running camp in Asheville, N.C. – God follows me there, too.
- Old bookstores, because I'm old school.
- Deep conversations with great friends.
- Plank, cobra, child's pose and bridge; meditations the way yoga was intended.
- Working six jobs at school, yet going to no meetings.
- Reading Harlan Coben mystery novels; humor and nostalgia with a twist at the end.
- Full tank of gas and an open road. Destination: who cares?
- Carpool, yes carpool. Because it's my first spiritual test of the day.
- The wisdom of saying nothing; walking away.
- Quiet time, this should be mandatory.
- Seeing the smiling face of a runner who just nailed it
- Cross country Saturday, followed by nap, followed by college football = YES!
- Sitting on the porch at my watering hole, the day complete.
- Tacos, two of them even; and spaghetti on a random Sunday.
- High school graduation; sitting in the audience with sensory overload, the introspective presence of every emotion.

- A scary movie on Halloween – because why not?
- Hiking, because nature provides many answers.
- The challenge of the blank page; life's adventures waiting to be written.
- Beach trips and mountain trips, and I couldn't care less which one.
- The continuing education of loving and being yourself; two challenges worth the effort
- And the 58th one, loving the fact that I could keep right on going.

Pep Rallies in Your Life

Most people have at least one memory of a high school pep rally, maybe more if they're lucky. One of my good friends was a high school football star at Clarkston in Atlanta; he once commented that nothing was like getting announced in front of a down South football crowd.

Personally, I can't imagine a much bigger high, unless perhaps you are a rock star about to grab the microphone in front of a packed house.

I wouldn't know in either case. My football days ended when I was knocked down by the tackling dummy... with nobody holding it. And I don't even sing in the shower in fear of the water turning off or going bad, whichever comes first.

In looking back, however, I do remember my one big moment. It was after we won the region basketball championship in 1977. We were pretty good, or at least we thought we were, and we had our trophy. So, one day, our headmaster called us all into the gym, sat us down by rows, grabbed the microphone. One by one, he called us all down. The "crowd" (I went to a VERY small school) clapped as we stood around center court.

However, that wasn't all. This team was going to be greeted with a special surprise!

Blindfolds were put over our eyes and someone from the crowd was going to come forward and give us a big kiss. Being fond of our cheerleaders, I had a crush on, well, pretty much all of them. Maybe it would be this one…maybe that one. In my case, I didn't care. I was about to be smooched by a real, live cheerleader. And with witnesses!

So, there I was. Smiling. Happy. On top of High School World. Bigger than life its own self. Then it happened: Someone walked forward and gave me a quick peck, nothing special. Man, was I disappointed! Where was my big kiss? Wasn't I a starting guard on this team? Where was the love? In the normal rollercoaster psyche of the teen-ager, I went from higher than the roof to lower than a street curb in seconds flat. Until they pulled the blindfold off…

There, right in front of me, stood my mother. Quite frankly, I'm not sure where my mood went at that point. After all, what do you say when you have a blindfold on and your mother sneaks out of the crowd and kisses you? I do remember being a bit relieved. After all, I didn't grab her and go for it. (Oh dear the thought…)

In moving forward, I just came from a pep rally, where I just saw the A-to-Z of being a teenager. Our dance team performed in front of a roaring crowd and a tremendous ovation. One of our football players was called down to participate in a water balloon toss and they butchered his name. Some had to play "Name That Tune" and finish a random song. Some of them walked away heroes. Others were laughing stocks of the day.

I stood off to the side, reminiscing, trying to imagine the mood swings that just happened within the last 74 seconds or so. Adrenaline. Pain. Embarrassment. Pride. Glory. Goat-hood.

I'm not the most astute person in the world, but I felt every bit of it. Still do as I'm pecking away at these keys. In fact, my face is turning red in shame while, at the same time, I'm strutting in front of my class like a peacock – the presence of all emotions. Part of me wants people to give me attention; the other part wants to pull covers over my eyes.

We deserve a pep rally every now and then, you know? Don't get me wrong, I'm all about doing unto others and putting ladies first and giving and shrugging away the credit and taking care of your brothers and sisters.

Still, there comes a time when you must prop yourself up at the end of the day, pour yourself the drink or your choosing and practically break your own arm patting your own self on the back. We're taught not to do that, you know? You should be ashamed of even thinking that, I was once told.

Nope, Wayne Dyer had it right. If you have no love from within or for yourself, then you simply have no love to give. What comes out comes from within. Period. No exceptions. After all, you're doing the best you can, right? God made you, correct? And He loves you, right? Why is He supposed to love you but you're not supposed to? Aren't you one of his creations? Did He make a mistake?

I don't think so – not in this world.

In wrapping this up, I look back on all my days of strutting and hiding. Of course, there are regrets, but I think we should take our love when we get it. In present day, I stand and applaud, pep rally after pep rally, honoring others and that is fine. Still, when the moon is tilted funny, I can't help think back of the few times I've been the one standing up front.

Yes, I deserved it. Sure, I felt honored. Yes, I felt the love. And yes, it was great!

Even if I did end up kissing my own mother.

Final Buzzer

Win or lose, senior cheerleader Amanda Gibson knew this was going to happen.

Get the picture: It's the state finals for the Holy Innocents' Golden Bear girls' basketball team in the Class A-Private classification at McCamish Pavilion at Georgia Tech. They are battling Wesleyan, they always seemed to be, and it was a close game as always.

"I wasn't even supposed to be there," Amanda recalled. "I was in Mexico on Spring Break. I told my mom that I would simply die if I weren't at that game. We changed plans, called the airport, made a flight out at 5 a.m."

Driving to the arena, the senior said she felt a funny feeling inside. "I started calling all my teammates; we talked about how this was going to be our last game together. We've made so many memories on those sidelines. And we are all so close; we've become like sisters."

For the record, there were 10 senior cheerleaders at courtside that day – the only exception was junior Josie Maxwell. And, also for the record, final buzzers are sad for all involved, regardless of the outcome. Parents die a slow death. The athlete celebrates or not, but eventually reflect. And the coaches play the game over in their heads.

True, it's never easy leaving the athletic facility when it's your last time. Sure, some will move on and play at the next level, but many will go home, wash their uniforms, and turn them in on Monday. They will lift the pressed-for-the-final-time garment and hand it to their coach, never to get to do so again. Their face may be plain, but their insides are churning times 50.

Besides, what do you say when you've just done something you'll never do again? Exactly what do you do with the pain; where do you put it, and how do you summarize something that's become a part of your life? Years on the sidelines are now down to one day, one game, and then, poof – it's gone. The career was both the wink of an eye and the longest days and nights of your life, often depending on your mood.

On this day, the fourth quarter rolls around. The cheerleaders are all grouped under the Holy Innocents' basket, pom-poms in hand, yelling for all they're worth. Any positive is a reason to jump and yell, get the fans involved, spur the players on. This is so tense, so exciting, and almost scary at times. They scream louder.

At around 3:20 on this day, however, the inevitable happens. A buzzer sounds in downtown Atlanta, a noise with a finality that will always be remembered. Our players huddle together while the opposition celebrates. Parents grab their stuff, coaches grab their clipboards, support staff meets to discuss the events. Writer's write; refs change back into their street clothes; the announcer reminds everybody to drive safely on the way home.

As for Amanda Gibson, she simply turns and faces her lifetime friend and teammate, Emmy Morgan. Without a word shared between them, they embrace and burst into tears.

Ode to All Graduates

May is approaching, and for the 11th consecutive year, I will pronounce myself officially sad. This marks the 11th straight year I've sat at Convocation back in August, the coach in me grabbing myself by the collar, and reminded myself I will NOT get too attached this year. Every year I tell myself this.

And every year I am wrong. Maybe next year I'll leave myself alone, let *me* be the one to get educated; allow myself to stroll, wander and bond with the blessed teens. After all, I'm fooling no one here, they're the ones teaching me. Trust me on that one.

In the halls and in my life, it's a thing I do now, after getting over my crap from years ago. I often check in with God, and yes I'm weird enough to hear His questions. Do you want to go into another line of work? Do you want to move someplace else? Are there other people you want to get involved with besides these? Aren't you getting tired of this depression?

And in these halls, in my life and even today, I look up and offer only one word: Noooo…

I could cite 126 examples of what this current bunch means to me. Instead, I'll share this: When these seniors were sophomores, one of the girl's dog was run over and killed. Her 18 classmates heard the news, huddled together in the middle of the class-room. "We're going to make her a video. You do the filming, you write the script, you guys make the cards."

This huddle resulted in a video that changed her tears from

189

sad to warm. I witnessed this and I'm a better man because of it. Many things we forget. This, I will not.

Because these are the things these kids do. When told to grow up as I often am, I want to say, "Grow up into what? Is there anything better than this? Grow into politics and rage and interest rates and phone bills? Or Trump versus Hillary? Really?"

I have Peter Pan Syndrome down to an art. In fact, I admire the character as much as I did Pistol Pete growing up. I thanked God for this just the other day. The sun peeked through a cloud as He let me know it's okay, I can freely admit this.

In moving on, a ceremony is forthcoming that will be way more than just something to sit through. It will remind me of my days attempting to be an athlete, while at the year-end banquets. There was one major thought: I SO wish I'd done more; wish I'd been better. Banquets, like graduations, are supposed to be celebrations. I find them both more soul-searching. I don't and won't apologize for that, either.

Yes, the Cosmic High School Dance is a slow process until, one day, you realize they've yet again pounded their way into your very soul. Maybe it hits you while you're loading the dishwasher, or listening to the traffic report, or sitting at your watering hole.

It happens every year, every time. I've read often, almost daily, about how you're not supposed to let others affect your mood – that it all comes from within. These kids trump that, and me, and on a daily basis. I'm not ashamed to admit that either.

I've scribbled long enough; have straightened my own collar; have said it the way I feel it, the way I know it. In looking over what I've said, the questions come at me again. Do you really want to publish this? Do you want to be this transparent regarding a bunch of kids? Do you live for this? Would you do it again?

And for the second time today, I look up and offer only one word. Yeeeesss!

And with that, He let me sleep.

Just My Opinion

- No human on Earth should ever say, "Don't you know who I am?"
- Naps should be incorporated into everyone's daily life, even at work if possible.
- Just because you said it to someone's face doesn't make it okay. Being mean is being mean. Period.
- The definition of pointless is when men are ripping on women or women ripping on men. It takes both to keep the world going, so there...
- Written by Charlie Reese: "Politicians are the only people who create problems and then campaign against them. If both democrats and republicans are against deficits, then why do we have deficits? If democrats and republicans are against inflation and higher taxes, then why do we have inflation and higher taxes." Hmm...
- The movies *I Can Only Imagine* and *Wonder* are both well-worth seeing. A quote from *Wonder:* It's hard to blend in when you're born to stand out.
- Still, 80s movies were the best – it's hard to top *Fast Times at Ridgemont High, Stripes, Caddyshack, Arthur, Ferris Bueller's Day Off, The Breakfast Club* and many more.

- I love watching football though grateful every day I never played it. Brain injuries and concussions are through the roof these days.
- Sometimes it's hard to beat a good plate of spaghetti, a smoothie or lemonade from Chick-fil-A. And I still miss my mom's ice tea.
- Something that just popped into my head – "If you're enjoying the tunnel, what difference does it make if there's light at the end of it or not?"
- People who complain are a turn off. We're the luckiest people who have ever lived.
- Written by Robert James Waller: "Self-important people are preposterous. We come, we do, we go, and we shouldn't take ourselves any more seriously than that."
- I'd rather have a 22-second conversation in the halls between classes with one of our kids than interview most any famous person in the country, with extremely few exceptions.
- I'd rather fold clothes than go to a regular season NBA game – regardless of who's playing.
- Most people over-sing the National Anthem.
- "Be brief, be brilliant, be gone" is the best advice I've ever gotten about public speaking. Even if you're rocking it, people are ready for you to sit down after the seven - or eight-minute mark.
- The Golden Rule is still simple, classic, and wonderful. It's called Golden for a reason.
- I close in gratitude. I can't think of too many places I'd rather be.

Subconsciously Speaking

It's 6:43 in the morning and I've already called myself so many names, even the casual, laid-back fellow would've taken me out back and pounded me into submission. Words and thoughts, one day I will learn, have lots of power.

After all, when it comes to memory, women and elephants have nothing on our subconscious minds; what we take in and accept are vital. I'm reminded of a scene in *Animal House*, when Dean Vernon Wormer told one of the fraternity brothers, "Drunk, fat and stupid are no way to go through life, son."

The guy then proceeded to puke on Dean Wormer, but you get the point.

It was Meister Eckhart who said that if you could only utter one prayer, a simple 'thank you' would suffice. Writer Kamal Ravikant went around repeating "I love myself" in his head, with miraculous results. Louise Hay was big on affirmations. And one Hawaiian tradition says you should repeat, "I'm sorry. Please forgive me. Thank you. I love you."

What I do know is this: drunk, fat and stupid doesn't work. Old, tired and bald doesn't do a lot of good, either; nor does poor, bored and mad. There's a whole list of sentiments, with "life's a bitch and then you die" perhaps the most common.

Interestingly, I told somebody one day about how I keep repeating 'thank you' while bored at carpool. He was flabbergasted. "But that's brainwashing!"

Exactly! That's my point! Besides, doesn't he realize how we've become negative in the first place? Newspapers. The news. Social media. Water cooler and locker room conversations.

Conclusion: The subconscious mind is neither forgiving nor unforgiving. It simply remembers. Period. Words have power, especially in my opinion when written. It's time to throw in something different, something happier, more positive, peaceful. Mental health, after all, is an important thing. People are shooting others, and themselves, at an alarming rate these days. If you want to get rich, start selling antidepressants.

Call me crazy. I'll take it as a compliment, but I'm going to go with this one for today: "Life is easy. It's an adventure. It's one simple, sacred story to write after another."

So, deal with that mind of mine. How's that for different? And thank you. Seriously, thank you.

Transformation Through Tennis

I'm done with tennis now, finished as a player, a fan, and a coach. Rarely do I speak of it; never do I watch it on TV. And not once have I missed it. I placed my rackets on the top shelf of my closet in 2014 and I don't think they've moved. Still, despite being on or around the courts for 45-plus years, I feel I still owe the game something, because there was a lot missing in my departure. It was so abrupt, like a snubbing, as if I never gave the game the respect it still deserves.

I have only one choice as I try to pay my karmic debt, both to my conscience and the game itself. I can only do it justice the way I know how – through the power of the written word. So, as briefly as I can tell it, this is what happened:

It was around 1975 and I was a Rutledge Academy Raider, trying to disguise myself as an athlete. With two Madison Open tennis championships under my belt (I think I got a bye to the finals both times), I proudly walked up to my Headmaster/tennis coach in the halls one day, mustered up the little nerve I had, and made my big announcement.

"Mr. Purcell, I am going on the tournament trail this summer. I'm going to get good and I'm going to play college tennis."

The old man sort of glanced at me out of the corner of his eye, grabbed me by my shoulder, gripped me tight if my memory serves, and said, "Come into my office, son. Sit down. Close the door."

As a 15-year-old, having your headmaster tell you to sit down and close the door is a very scary thing. It produces a fast heart rate, sweating, perhaps an unplanned bowel movement. Still, we won't go there.

"I'm going to tell you two things right now," he said, staring at me from across that big, shiny desk of his. "Number one, you are about to meet the best people you've ever met in your life."

Awesome, I thought. This is great! Not only will I be catching a good tan, playing some tennis, and traveling around, but I'm going to meet great people! "What's the second thing?" I asked.

"Number two," he answered. "You're about to meet the biggest horses' asses you've ever met in your life."

My heart sank. Jesus wept. The crowd returned to their seats. The up-and-down life of a teenager just went down. There I sat, all confused.

Confused, young, and stupid.

Regardless, off I went, traveling from city to city, chasing down fuzzy, optic yellow tennis balls. And I took it seriously! In fact, my mood would often depend on where those balls landed, or in some cases, didn't land on those courts. Wherever I was, however, my headmaster's words never left me. Never. In between all the days of cross courts, down the lines, first serve wide, approach to the corner, volley into the open court, I always heard the mantra – great people…horses' butts…great people…horses' butts.

The result? I traveled everywhere attracting both. On a good day, my opponent and I would shake hands after a match, go off and grab a beer or two, continue into the night and get rejected with the best of them by the female players on the circuit.

On a bad day, there'd be line judges, officials, parents, controversy. In fact, sometimes I'd seen fewer adults at a crime scene.

Rackets would fly, profanity filled the air, warnings would be administered, fierce looks would exchange across the nets.

Through it all, I never knew you attracted what you thought about, what you focus on becomes your reality. And me, I knew only two kinds of tennis players so, by God, that's what I attracted.

Whenever I met a player, in fact, if they didn't seem like they were very nice, then they were – by process of elimination – horses' butts. They had to be, right? I never had a clue that some, if not most, could be somewhere in between.

And so the story went... for probably 40-plus years.

Now don't get me wrong, I've got my good memories – great ones even. If my house burned down today, I wouldn't hesitate to call the likes of a Skip Johnson out in Newnan or a Pride Evans down in St. Simons and they'd take care of me in a flash. Just last month, in fact, I commiserated with a college teammate and helped him through a mini-depression. When I was in a funk 10 years ago, it was primarily tennis people who helped pull me through.

To this day, my cell phone is filled with the numbers of most of my college teammates; even more with coaches I've come across through ALTA and USTA and the like.

Perhaps the best of the best, however, happened in my tennis coaching days at Holy Innocents'. One of my players – I won't mention any names but his initials are Camiren Carter – was in a dispute with his opponent. The dispute? Camiren was arguing the score in his opponent's favor! "No," he said. "I'm not up 3-2, YOU are up 3-2. You won that game!"

I was so impressed I never stopped telling that story. I told it to one rival coach so many times he walked out between changeovers and shook Camiren's hand. (Great guy)! Another coach was so impressed he tried to recruit the kid away from me. (See? A horses' butt!)

At the banquet that spring, when usually the names of the award winners are kept in suspense, I made Camiren stand in front of our cafeteria, filled with 200-plus, and I told that story. I made every eye in that place go to him, watched, and appreciated while the lad got a tad nervous; got weepy-eyed myself when telling all those people what that young man did. Yes, I embarrassed him but, you know what? I'd do it again. Tennis takes enough beating for the "bad boys" of the game. I love that kid for what he did on that court that day. I'm getting a little weepy eyed, in fact, just writing about it.

He's somewhere in Connecticut now; he had to transfer out because of his dad's job. Wherever he is, whatever he's become, I hope he doesn't change. Ever.

But let's get to match point: Fast forward to 2014, my last year of coaching tennis. I'd gone into my AD's office and told her Dunn was done. I was filling out my last month, on cruise control, before riding off into the sunset – or perhaps the rain.

It was a nice spring day, similar to the one 42 years ago when I got up the nerve to make my big announcement to my coach. As fate would have it, because God really does keep score and He really does have a great sense of humor, one of my players walked up to me, grabbed me by the arm, said he wanted to talk. "I'm thinking about playing tournaments this summer," he said. "I want to get good; maybe play in college."

Goose bumps went up and down my arms. My hair stood up in the back (and it was actually one of my few good hair days). I recalled that conversation all those years ago oh so vividly. A smile crossed my face; my heart felt warm and I got all gooey inside. "Come into my office," I said. "Sit down, close the door."

He looked a little surprised. After all, not many people at my work have seen me get serious very often.

He was tall and thin and gangly, as they all seem to be – all angles and elbows. He sat; looked up at me expectantly. Me, I was deliberate. I knew what I had to do; couldn't wait to do it even. I walked across that room to where he was sitting, extended my hand, offered it right in front of him, and said, "Congratulations!"

Confused, he shook my hand, looked up and asked, "What are you congratulating me for?"

"Because," I said, "you're about to meet the best people you've ever met in your life."

Game. Set. Match.

In Defense of the High School Kid

It often pushes my buttons when I see and hear adults throw up their arms and say something like "Kids these days!" Hmm, wonder where they get this from? And while we're talking about the kids these days, let's take one I worked with, just for an example. Here is a day in her life:

Up at 5:30 in the morning, studying

Shower and off to school, class from 8:30 a.m. – 3 p.m. with a break for lunch

Cross country practice, 3:45 – 5:45

Dinner, shower, "me" time – 6 – 7 p.m.

Study – 7:30 to midnight

Sleep -????

Get the picture: During that day, she had to please two parents, five teachers, three coaches, one advisor, two siblings, and, let's not forget, herself. Keep in mind, we're talking about minds still in its early years – the axons not all firing or perhaps they're firing too much.

In addition, throw in texting, tweeting and other social media, so you can add massive peer pressure and too much information, causing many reasons for confusion. I wrote about one day in spring – April 20th.

Our job in all this? We are bumpers on a bumper pool table,

and our job is to keep these students in the game; on the board, not off to the side. ("Off to the side", in my opinion, is why we have school shootings, mental troubles, bullying issues.)

Some of us aren't mainstream. I had a conversation with my doctor yesterday; he said something that stuck out. "I wasn't one of the cool kids, but you know what? I think that helps makes us nicer people as we grow up." I like that. It gives you a view from the middle. You're not at the top or the bottom, but you're close enough to both sides to give a good perspective.

Finally, I think often the best advice, when you don't know what to say, is to simply suggest they get more rest. Lack of sleep snowballs, and in a very bad way.

This can prove huge.

I will go now. Must wait for the results from yesterday's physical. Have some issues to take care of. I will wait in lines at the bank, dodge Atlanta traffic and deal with the public. It always fascinates me, seeing the people who feel they're too good to wait in line, those who get surly with the tellers or the check-out people.

Who do they think they are? Don't they know we're all in this together? Don't they realize that only a small percentage –as in the movie *Grease* – got to meet an Olivia Newton John and dance on top of cars in joy. And the only time I've ever danced on top of a car it was highly suggested I get down and quick. Why don't we care more?

Oh, well, you know how those adults are…

Rock Bottom, Then Up Again

(Ode to a Depression)

Eleven years ago –

JUNO BEACH, FL - When you walk out of Running Sports and hang a right, there's a bench that sits there, halfway between the store and Dunkin Donuts. No real description needed, it's just a bench.

A group of about 20 of us had just completed a 10-mile run that spanned from Running Sports, past the ocean, down to Jupiter Island and back to Running Sports. When you pass the sea on the way back, the early hour gives you a view of the sun rising. It's beautiful times 12 and is a reminder that, regardless of what you're going through, there's a wonderful synchronicity to this thing called life. Watching a sunrise can remind you of that.

Anyway, this day the run has ended; I'm sitting on that bench. We had talked for a while after the run – some of us went into Dunkin Donuts, some loitered in the parking lot, others ventured away quietly. Eventually the 20 of us became 14, then 8, then 5, then me…It was just me, sitting on that bench.

The depression struck again as it often did, mostly without warning but this time very painful. After all, I had nowhere to go. No job to speak of, no wife, no life, no kids to tend to. I felt like Forrest Gump sitting there that day, except at least Forrest

Gump had a feather floating down from above, it's aimless pattern representing his random adventures that would take him wherever the wind blew.

I looked up, almost in tears. No damn feather no damn where to be seen. It was just me. On a bench. In a place I hadn't been able to make it successfully and call home.

Two weeks earlier, you see, I'd taken a test. It was a 40-point test and, unlike all other tests I'd taken in my life, this one I wanted, actually needed, to score low on. After all, if you scored more than 10, you were depressed.

I made a 22. Even the doctor was impressed. "Wow," he said under his breath. I probably wasn't supposed to hear that but I did. And I would say it ticked me off, but when you're depressed, little things like that go WAY into the backburner and off the grid. So be it.

That day eventually passed, they usually do. And then another, and another. Quite frequently I would get hit with what I would later call "crap storms," ones that drive you to simply lie down or sit. Despite all the books, tapes, and videos out there about depression, I can still sum it up in one word: Paralyzing! It's mentally and physically paralyzing.

Here's an example: Even the thought of going to Kroger would make my mind go something like this: Oh my God! I'm going to have to get up, get dressed, get in the car which takes gas which takes money which I don't have. Then I'm going to have to get out, in public, and maybe have to talk to people!

That's not exactly correct, but you see? The thought of doing ANYTHING will cause the mind to throw in a top-40 list of why you can't and shouldn't do it.

In moving on, one day, a week or so later, I'd had enough. I looked up, made up my mind, dug in my heels, threw up my fists at any God up there who could take a moment to listen and I said this: "Please don't take my irreverence as disrespect, I'm not very good at this. If you know me, you've probably heard I've pretty much been an irresponsible, crazy guy for most of my life. But here's my deal with you: I ask that each tomorrow be a little bit better than each today – whatever the degree. In return, I promise to do at least ONE thing every day to get myself closer to what I want to become. It may be something small, it may not end up mattering, but I will do at least one thing. Thanks for listening. Peace out."

So there, I said it. I had my deal with the Universe. Being someone who'd often reneged on promises and projects in my past, this however would be different. I would see this through and if I died trying, so dang what?

And so it began: I became Ahab chasing the whale. I'd read somewhere that in life, we all need three things: Something to do, something to love and something to look forward to. Currently I was 0-for-3 and heading back to the minors.

Still, I began to dig, tossing out as much dirt and crap from my head as I possibly could, one shovel load at a time. In retrospect, my thoughts – as they usually are – were probably backwards. Life, you see, will teach you to work on your weaknesses. I in this case respectfully disagree. I think you should work on your strengths, develop them further. After all, you're not going to make a living doing things you don't like or don't care about. Are you?

I had my plan. What should I do? Read. Write. Run. Everything else is pretty much a distraction. And I knew where I wanted to do it. Whether it took a day, a year or five, I was going home to my old job back at this place called Holy Innocents'; a place I'd always been most happy. Just watch.

The Universe listened, sent me signs, answered. I made phone calls, sent emails, made an uninvited nine-hour drive to Atlanta. The headmaster there asked me point blank, once he figured he wasn't ever going to get rid of me, "Where else have you applied?"

"Nowhere," I quickly answered. "I'm going to work here." His eyes rose, lowered again. I wasn't supposed to see or notice that. I did. It was happening.

It took me six months. The final word, I was told, was that only one available job existed at the school...a secretarial position. I took it.

For the 2007-2008-school year, I proceeded to be perhaps the worst secretary – oops, I mean administrative assistant – this world has ever known. Still, some "luck" came my way. The cross country coach left at the last minute – he also coached tennis. One of the public relations people moved out of state. I kept my promise to God: One thing every day. Read. Write. Run.

It's not the big things in life, it's the little ones, all added up, that make lifetimes worth talking about at parties or in break rooms at work. In the days ahead, it took one kid at a time...one cross country meet at a time...one story at a time...one class at a time. But it worked. Bad days became mediocre became decent became good. Crap storms became less often; they weren't as intense when they hit. One day I looked around and all was great. I was writing stories, coaching cross country and tennis, being with kids in the classroom. Things were so good I began to walk in fear of when the other shoe was going to drop.

I had asked and I continue to do so. The Universe kept sending me signs. As Martin Luther King once said, "You don't have to see the whole staircase, just take the first step." Thank you, Dr. King; I can't tell you how much I've needed that.

Present day:

ATLANTA, GA - I'm finishing up a run at the Chattahoochee River. It's a beautiful, fall day. The leaves are throwing colors at me I've not seen before. The trail is soft enough to be easy on my legs, the mile markers are slowly disappearing behind my feet and I can't help but smile as I see the sun set to my left behind the river.

My shoe comes untied, so I stopped to sit at a nearby but convenient bench. With my back to the water, my mind zoomed backwards over the past 11 years. Please hear me: My thoughts then were not and aren't of boasting, of a "ha-ha I did it" type nature. Being an almost elderly soul I understand how quickly the trap door can open, how loved ones die, things happen.

Still, I have to laugh. After all, why just in the last couple years some of the craziest stuff imaginable has happened. The Cubs won the World Series; Donald Trump is President, my friend Phil Wendel – the untrappable point guard – got married. I laugh at my past, this present, the possibilities and how the fact remains – if you want guarantees in life then, quite simply, you don't want life.

I laugh out loud. People passing by stare at me and think me odd. I am. I laugh again in agreement and so what? As if on cue, I look up and see a leaf falling off a branch, weaving in the wind, heading my way.

I don't even wait for it to land. Instead I get up and finish my run.

Dunn Neugebauer
Fall 2016 – Summer 2018

About the Author

Dunn Neugebauer is one of the few who managed to live the undergrad college experience twice; once at Berry College and again as an adult while working at Oglethorpe University. He worked for several newspapers along the way, most notably the Palm Beach Post, the Tampa Tribune, and the Marietta Daily Journal. In 2012, his first book, "Funny Conversations with God – an Uncalled-for Dialogue," was published. Now working at Holy Innocents' Episcopal School in Atlanta, Neugebauer holds many jobs, some of which include communications, carpool, subbing in the Upper School, coaching cross country and track, and monitoring the halls when time allows. This is his first collection of essays.